PRAISE FOR
THE POWER OF FORGIVENESS

"The Power of Forgiveness by Ronald H. Bartalini is a Life changing book, for myself! I was impressed so much with the research and well thought out examples and true life stories it contains. Once I commenced to read I could not lay this most interesting read aside until I had finished it. It is the kind of book that one must keep close by as a guide for one's life challenges day to day." **David M. Jarvis, Owner & C E O of Valley View Electric & Engineering, Former Director of Maintenance & Facility Management for the State of Utah**

"The first time I read Ronald H. Bartalini's new book, "The Power of Forgiveness, I went off to find a quiet place to read one chapter. Once I had read the book in depth I found many different connotations that genuinely affected my life in a positive way. I have just finished my third reading and I have continued to find new insights that are helpful."
R. Nelson, Salesman

"The Power of Forgiveness" by Ronald H. Bartalini has arrived. This little book inspires, verifies, and guides one to the reality of the power of forgiveness. Beautiful insights. Creditable foundations. Tangible processes. Excellent read." **Darla Salin, International author's assistant**

"What a great book! The Power of Forgiveness by Ronald H. Bartalini is a book that can teach all of us, even the most hardened soul, how to seek and obtain forgiveness by forgiving others. Through contemporary inspiring stories and examples from scripture, the author walks us through how we can find joy, affirmation, and peace by following the example of the Savior by loving and forgiving unconditionally. He reminds us that we all have need of forgiveness and to receive forgiveness we must be willing, humble, and forgiving of those who have wittingly or unwittingly wronged us. This at times can be a difficult task. However, the author in a succinct, and in an entertaining manner instructs how this can be done on a daily basis and in the process changes us and makes us into the people that God wants us to be."

Gary Crawford, DDS, Oral and Maxillofacial Surgeon

The *POWER*
of
FORGIVENESS

RONALD H. BARTALINI

Sundie Enterprises
Since 1972

Cover art, Statue by: Bernardelli, Christo.
From Wikipedia, Used by Permission.

ISBN#978-0-9859811-8-1
Library of Congress Catalogue Number:
2016909054

Description: This book will show you how to
allow those bitter feelings of being used, taken
advantage of, offended or persecuted go away
and learn how to forgive the offender. You will
learn how to ask forgiveness of those you may
have offended. Best of all, you will learn how to
forgive yourself.

1. Self Help 2. Inspirational 3.Motivational
1. Bartalini, Ronald H.

Published by:
Sundie Enterprises
P.O. Box 1274
Provo, Utah 84603-1274

Dedication

For all, who truly want to learn how to: forgive. For all who wish to have the courage to ask forgiveness of those they may have offended. And finally, for the man or woman who truly wants to learn how to forgive-themselves.

Acknowledgments

I am grateful to my friend and neighbor,
Bill Baker for his encouragement for this work.

Preface

How can power be attached to the act of forgiveness? There is great power in this process because forgiving another softens the heart of the oppressor. When one asks forgiveness of another, that act of contrition softens the heart of the one who is the offender and not surprisingly, it softens the heart of whoever asks forgiveness of another.

Forgiveness or the act of forgiving another their trespasses against you is more powerful than Superman, Batman, Iron Man, Captain America and Spider Man, even all of those "fictional" super heroes combined. In the real world, forgiveness is more powerful than a hydrogen bomb or the most powerful nuclear warhead because although these have great destructive power they cannot cause our Heavenly Father to forgive us of our sins.

In addition to this, I find only one place in all of scripture where Jesus spells out clearly what is required of us to have our Heavenly Father forgive us of our trespasses. The Lord promises us in his wonderful Sermon on the Mount, "For if you forgive men their trespasses, your heavenly Father will also forgive you" (Matthew 6:14).

Stop the presses! Here is one thing that all of mankind can do and if we do it we have the Savior's promise that our Heavenly Father, will forgive us of our trespasses. Now comes that principle and truth which is so seldom spoken of that it may as well be thought of as a secret. The Master then counsels:

"But if you forgive not men their trespasses neither will your Father forgive your trespasses" (Matthew 6:15).

The word trespasses is another way of saying, "sins." Therefore, if we do not first forgive others their sins against us, our Heavenly Father will not forgive us for our sins. This paints a different picture than you will have perhaps had before understanding this truth. Jesus is teaching us that we must "first forgive" if we hope to be forgiven by God.

Forgiving another gives us a kind of insurance policy that if we forgive, we will also be forgiven by the Father for our trespasses.

Next time you hear someone preaching what one must do to get to heaven be certain to listen for this truth and hope that they have it at the top of their list. Forgiveness is a tonic to the oppressor. Forgiveness lightens the heart of the vengeful. When a man asks forgiveness of one he has wronged, that act of contrition softens the heart of him who is asking forgiveness. Forgiveness allows the angels to record the forgiver's name in the Lamb's Book of Life.

If you ever hope to acquire wisdom and understanding you will have to get a handle on forgiveness. Forgiveness is not a one-sided coin. Forgiveness has many facets. Each part of forgiveness is worthy of our careful attention.

The principle of forgiveness is made up of three basic parts. From his Sermon on the Mount the Savior first teaches us to ask forgiveness of all those we may have offended. We read, "Therefore if thou bring thy gift to the altar, and there rememberest that thy brother hath ought against thee; Leave there thy gift before the altar, and go thy way; first be reconciled to thy brother, and then come and offer thy gift" (Matthew 5:23-34).

What does the word, *reconciled* mean? From Webster's Dictionary we read, Reconciliation is, "The act of reconciling, or the state of being reconciled; reconcilement; restoration to harmony; renewal of friendship." Therefore, if you know you have offended a friend or neighbor because of something you have said or done or something you may have left undone, it now falls upon you to go to your friend that you know has been offended and apologize to him or her and make things right.

Continuing with his sermon to all of mankind the Son of God mentions his Father when he instructs us to forgive all those who have trespassed against us. Finally, we ultimately learn that we must forgive ourselves for the transgressions we commit in this life.

Which of these three will be the most difficult to accomplish? The answer may vary for everyone. However, all of this can only be accomplished by and through the atonement of Jesus Christ. In today's popular culture we have people saying in books, movies and song lyrics, "I will be my own Savior," but the truth is, no one can save himself. Jesus Christ is the only name given under heaven whereby men and women can be saved. (Acts 4:12). There simply is no other way and no other name given.

We can only be saved by and through the perfect and infinite atonement of Jesus Christ. I believe this is also the key to accessing the power and ability to achieve victory over all three parts making up the principle of forgiveness. With the atonement and grace of Jesus Christ we can do all things but without our Lord and Savior, we will be left on our own to stumble.

He who can forgive has mercy written on his heart and the light of truth in his heart. The act of forgiveness is nothing less than a magnificent display of that which the Father would have all of his children do to eventually become perfect, even as he is perfect. When the Savior of the world hung on the cross at Calvary and said, "Father forgive them for they know not what they do" (Luke 23:34), Jesus was showing us what he meant when he said, "The Father hath not left me alone; because I do only those things that please him" (John 8:29).

If the Son of God could forgive those who dishonored him, tortured him, and took his life, can we who claim to love the Savior of the world do any less?

The Process

Is there a process to follow if you hope to be forgiven by God? I believe there is. We can see this series of changes unfold in the life of John Newton, the author of the world famous hymn, "Amazing Grace." When his ship was caught in a storm threatening to destroy all on board, Newton prayed to God and promised that if God would save him, he would serve God for the rest of his life. Please notice that there is another aspect to being forgiven by God and being able to forgive another that is perhaps not spoken of enough. That is, acknowledging that you are a sinner. Here is John Newton's story:

John Newton

John Newton did not just wake up one morning and write, "Amazing grace how sweet the sound that saved a wretch like me." First, that man had to become a wretch. He had to become miserable even as Jean Valjean. Both men had to have their own individual epiphanies and acknowledge that they were miserable, wretched and sinners, before God could work in their lives, lift them up, and make new men of them.

By his early twenties, Newton had become a rebellious person. Even the toughest sailors, known for their cursing and drinking, were sickened by Newton's foul language. He refused to follow the captain's orders and constantly made fun of anyone who believed in God. When he remembered what his mother taught him, he would try to be good, but his efforts would only last a short time. (Christianity.com)

When a violent storm in 1748 battered his vessel off the coast of County Donegal, Ireland, and threatened to destroy all onboard, the crew manned the pumps and fought the storm for 11 days. Newton tied himself to the mast and steered the ship from one o'clock until midnight.

He had ridden out many a fierce storm before, but never had he come this close to death. As the ship began to break into pieces and water rushed in everywhere, one sailor washed overboard. A few hours later when Newton faced certain death, he began to recall Bible verses his mother had taught him. Newton, who couldn't swim, heard himself cry, "Lord, have mercy on us." But then he thought, "What mercy can there be for a wretch like me?" As he began to tell God he was sorry for turning away from Him and for doing so much wrong, he began to feel peace in his soul. (Christianity.com).

Newton eventually called out to God for mercy, and God saved John Newton. Just as God saved Peter from sinking into the billowing deep when Peter's faith failed him for fear of the violent storm that raged around him.

Jesus saved Newton from being a wretch and Jesus saved the apostle Peter from his doubts. That is what Christ does. Jesus lifts all men who reach out to him and saves all men who reach up to him. The Savior has told us, "For God sent not his Son into the world to condemn the world: but that the world through him might be saved" (John 3:17).

But when Newton called out to God for mercy in 1748, his faith in God was just beginning. While his boat was being repaired in Lough Swilly, Ireland, having been saved from the threat of drowning at sea, Newton took time to pen the words of the first verse of, "Amazing Grace."

Once he was safe; Newton quickly forgot God and went on with his life of being a slave trader. He continued his slave trading until 1754 or 1755, when he ended his seafaring altogether and began studying Christian theology. But from 1748 until 1754 or 1755 Newton resisted God. He had yet to fully commit himself to following the Savior.

Jesus may have spoken to Newton's heart at some point saying, "But you don't listen to me. It is hard for me to get your attention. Look what I have done for you. I have given you my words, words that will become the most well loved hymn of the modern age. Will you not embrace my words, words that have become your words? "Amazing grace, how sweet the sound, that saved a wretch like me. I once was lost but now am found, was blind but now I see." Will you not surrender your life to me? Will you not serve others and bring them to me? How can you continue to make your living in the slave trade? How can you continue to profit by allowing my children to suffer? Do you not remember calling out to me when your life was in peril and you were about to perish with your ship surrounded by the raging sea?"

Something must have stirred in Newton's heart and he was perhaps then able to call up ancient stirrings of when he lived with his Father in heaven. In that moment, he called out to God for mercy. The Savior may have then continued to speak to Newton's heart, "I reached out my arm and saved you then, just as I reached out my arm and saved Peter as his faith failed him and he began to sink into the deep as the storm raged around him. You have had your awakening. You have had your epiphany. You know it is I who saved your physical self. Will you now allow God to save your immortal soul? Will you allow God to save your soul by the atonement of Jesus Christ and by the grace of Christ? Will the words you have written remain only empty words?"

Christ calls out to all of his children, "Will you not hear my voice?" "Behold, I stand at the door, and knock: If any man will hear my voice, and open the door, I will come in to him, and will sup with him, and he with me" (Revelation 3:20). "Take my yoke upon you, and learn of me; for I am meek and lowly in heart: and ye shall find rest unto your souls. For my yoke is easy, and my burden is light" (Matthew 11:29-30).

But we not only need to listen and then hear; we also need to act. Newton did eventually act. "He became ordained as an evangelical Anglican cleric and served Olney, Buckinghamshire for two decades." (From Wikipedia, the free encyclopedia).

The Slave Trade

John Newton made many trips to Africa to buy slaves, who were sold in the United States and the Caribbean. Even after becoming a Christian, Newton did not see anything wrong with slavery, like most others during his time. Later Newton did begin to see that slavery was wrong. He and a young politician named William Wilberforce joined others who spoke out against the practice. In time their efforts led to a law, which banned slavery in England. (Christianity.com)

This epiphany, this awakening of the conscience of man to acknowledge that he is in fact a sinner and that he has wronged another, must happen first. Before a man can feel compassion for those he has wronged and before he can feel sorry for his mistakes he must ask forgiveness of those he has wronged. *All this must come before the sinner can ask God to forgive him, and certainly before he can forgive himself.*

So if you ever hope to get to that place in your life where you can forgive others, you must first acknowledge that you are a sinner. But don't let that fact disturb you too much because we are all sinners. "For all have sinned and come short of the glory of God" (Romans 3:23*). There is only one perfect man who has walked the earth and that is the Son of the living God, even Jesus Christ.*

Today, *Amazing Grace* is performed more than 10 million times each year! Can you listen to that hymn and not feel the love of God and the grace of God for all men? John Newton is not the only man who has acknowledged that he is a sinner. Although a fictional character, Jean ValJean from Victor Hugo's immortal "Les Miserables" already referred to, has also done the same.

Jean Valjean

Although this central character, Jean Valjean, is fictional in Hugo's Les Miserables, the timeless themes of redemption, compassion, mercy and Christ-like love explored by Hugo, have never been more relevant.

In this masterpiece, Hugo writes: "[Valjean] strained his eyes in the distance and called out . . . "Petit Gervais! His cries died away into the mist, without even awaking an echo . . .

His knees suddenly bent under him, as if an invisible power suddenly overwhelmed him with the weight of his bad conscience; he fell exhausted . . . and cried out, "I'm such a miserable man!"

"Valjean's encounter with Petit Gervais in Book Two of "Fantine" is the first interaction Valjean has after he leaves Myriel's house in Digne. Valjean's inability to keep his promise to become an honest man makes him realize how immoral he has become. Hugo's language in this passage emphasizes the gravity of this realization and portrays Valjean as physically collapsing under the weight of his conscience.

The desolate setting in which Valjean's epiphany takes place reflects the extent to which he has isolated himself from others. Valjean receives no response when he pleads for forgiveness, not even his own echo. The desolation also suggests that there is an emptiness in Valjean's soul, which he does not realize until his encounter with Myriel.

This emptiness is expressed by Valjean when he calls himself "miserable," a word that connotes both wretched behavior and unhappiness. For the first time in nearly two decades, Valjean acknowledges his transgressions. By doing so, he is finally able to feel compassion for his victim and recognize his own unhappiness. This scene marks the crucial turning point in Valjean's life, in which he begins to transform himself from a thief into a philanthropist." (From www.sparknotes.com).

When Valjean recognizes the emptiness in his soul and calls himself miserable, he is really saying, "I am a sinner." The reader has also been given an insight as to why the title of Hugo's masterwork is called, "Les Miserables," the words translate as "The Miserable."

Acknowledge That You Are a Sinner

When one acknowledges he is a sinner, he has done two things. He has not only admitted that he has sinned, he has also acknowledged that there is a God. Now that man can come to know Jesus Christ is the Savior of all mankind.

One of the first steps in the process of being forgiven by God is for a man to admit that he is a sinner. And for those who do so, you are not alone. As previously noted, we are all sinners. "For all have sinned and come short of the glory of God" (Romans 3:23).

Jesus rescues sinners and changes their lives into productive lives. That is what Jesus does.

The Publican

There was a certain publican who was able to confess in public that he was a sinner. Said he, "God be merciful to me a sinner" (Luke 18:13). We have the New Testament story from the gospel of Luke about this man.

"Two men went up into the temple to pray; the one a Pharisee, and the other a publican. The Pharisee stood and prayed thus with himself; God, I thank thee, that I am not as other men are, extortioners, unjust, adulterers, or even as this publican. I fast twice in the week, I give thee of all that I possess. *And the publican standing afar off, would not lift up so much as his eyes unto heaven, but smote upon his breast, saying God be merciful to me a sinner. (Luke 18:10-13).*

Forgiving Others Is Necessary Before God Can Forgive Us

The ability to forgive another person is absolutely necessary if we expect our Heavenly Father to forgive us. When Jesus gave us "the Lord's Prayer" he said, "And forgive us our debts as we forgive our debtors" (Matthew 6:12). Then the Lord promises as previously noted, "For if you forgive men their trespasses, your heavenly Father will also forgive you" (Matthew 6:14). "But if you forgive not men their trespasses neither will your Father forgive your trespasses" (Matthew 6:15).

When we develop the capacity to forgive, everything in our life changes. We slowly become more kind and humble, more teachable and child-like. One can even become more compassionate and giving.

When we learn to forgive we are becoming sculptors of our own marble statues just as Michelangelo sculpted and freed the living image he saw within the marble he sculpted. We are freeing the inner creation within ourselves and allowing that spirit within each man and woman to grow to fruition and reach its full potential.

How then do we acquire the virtue of being able to forgive another for their trespasses against us? I believe the answers can be found in the third chapter of Proverbs as follows:

The Importance of Mercy

The first thing wise old Solomon asks us to do is this, "Let not mercy and truth forsake thee: bind them about thy neck; write them upon the table of thine heart: so shall thou find favor and good understanding in the sight of God and man" (Proverbs 3:3-4).

What is mercy? From Webster's dictionary first published in 1828 we read, "That benevolence, mildness or tenderness of heart which disposes a person to overlook injuries, or to treat an offender better than he deserves; the disposition that tempers justice, and induces an injured person to forgive trespasses and injuries and to forbear punishment, or inflict less than law or justice will warrant.

In this sense, there is perhaps no word in our language precisely synonymous with mercy. That which comes nearest to it is grace. It implies benevolence, tenderness, mildness, pity or compassion, and clemency, but exercised only towards offenders. Mercy is a distinguishing attribute of the Supreme Being."

Jesus lists mercy as one of the beatitudes within his Sermon on the Mount. The Lord said, "blessed are the merciful: for they shall obtain mercy" (Matthew 5:7). I find it interesting that the Lord has said we must first be merciful if we are to obtain mercy. It is also interesting to me that our Savior tells us we must first forgive others, if we expect our Heavenly Father to forgive us. I believe that acquiring mercy also precedes being able to forgive.

Saul of Tarsus

What was lacking in Saul's life that could cause him to persecute the church of God and even condone the stoning death of Stephen who was one of the seventy and a minister of the Son of God? I suggest that which was missing in Saul's life was mercy and truth. Jesus began his Sermon on the Mount by naming the "merciful" among the blessed.

Saul did not simply need more mercy, he was completely void of it for no man with a modicum of mercy in his heart could so behave.

The Apostle Paul

By his own admission, the Apostle Paul called himself, *chief of sinners.* "This is a faithful saying and worthy of all acceptation, that Christ Jesus came into the world to save sinners; of of whom I am chief" (1 Timothy 1:15).

Saul Was a Terrorist of His Time

Saul of Tarsus was a Roman citizen by birth, by which he was exempted from all trials. (From the Lex Porcia, B.C. 247). Roman citizens, were exempted from degrading punishment such as flogging. (Acts 16:37). Being a Roman citizen allowed him to move about with impunity and to wreak havoc on the Church of God and all Christians.

Saul of Tarsus did not just hate Christians; he thought he was doing God service by disposing of them all. "He made it his goal to capture, then bring Christians to public trial and execution. Saul was present when the first Christian martyr (named Stephen) was killed by an angry mob. "... they all rushed at him (Stephen), dragged him out of the city and began to stone him. Meanwhile, the witnesses laid their clothes at the feet of a young man named Saul. . . And Saul was there, giving approval to his death" (Acts 7.57; 8:1). After Stephen was martyred, Saul went door to door in Jerusalem finding people who believed that Jesus is the Messiah. "Saul began to destroy the Church. Going from house to house, he dragged off men and women and put them in prison" (Acts 8:3). After putting these people in prison, Saul learned about their Christian friends in Damascus by somehow getting letters from the prisoners. "I persecuted the followers of this Way to their death, arresting both men and women and throwing them into prison, as also the high priest and all the Council can testify. I even obtained letters from them to their brothers in Damascus, and went there to bring these people as prisoners to Jerusalem to be punished" (Acts 22:4-5). (From Wikipedia, the free encyclopedia).

Jesus Forgave
Saul of Tarsus

But Christ forgave Saul to set forth a pattern that all who believe on him, can be saved, even the worst sinners. Paul continued to explain, "Howbeit for this cause I obtained mercy, that in me first Jesus Christ might shew forth all longsuffering for a pattern to them which should hereafter believe on him to life everlasting" (1 Tim: 1:16).

Saul's Early History

He received his education from Gamaliel the most famous of all Jewish Rabbis. "Under Gamaliel I was thoroughly trained in the law of our fathers and was just as zealous for God as any of you" (Acts 22:3). He spoke both Hebrew and Greek but his preferred language was Greek.

"He was from a devout Pharisaic Judean family of Benjaminite descent in the city of Tarsus–one of the largest trade centers on the Mediterranean coast. It had been in existence several hundred years prior to his birth. It was renowned for its university. During the time of Alexander the Great, who died in 323 BC, Tarsus was the most influential city in Asia Minor. Paul referred to himself as being "of the stock of Israel, of the tribe of Benjamin, a Hebrew of the Hebrews; as touching the law, a Pharisee" (Philippians 3:5). (From Wikipedia).

The Transformation of Saul of Tarsus

Jesus did for Saul that which he did for Peter. He changed a doubting heart into a believing heart. He reached down and lifted Saul up and forever changed him. He transformed a misguided soul into a productive one. While on the road to Damascus Saul saw a light and heard a voice from heaven. But what he saw was no ordinary light and what he heard was not an ordinary voice. Saul of Tarsus saw and heard the resurrected Son of God. Saul saw and heard he who had conquered death. Saul saw and heard the resurrected Savior of the world. Did he fall to his knees then and beg for forgiveness for persecuting and even consenting to the death of the Savior's followers? Did the very marrow in his bones come close to melting from the brightness of the risen Lord's glory? Did he see all the creations of God, as did Abraham and Moses? Did he then know and understand, that he was being spoken to by he who had created the world and all things; throughout the universe, including his then unworthy self?

Did Saul then say, help me to make right all the harm that I have done? Help me to correct all the pain and suffering I have caused? What did Jesus say to Saul upon revealing himself to him? Did he say, Saul you have persecuted those who have believed in me and for that you must suffer? Did the Son of God call down fire from heaven to destroy him? No. Jesus said, "Saul, Saul, why persecutest thou me, it is hard for thee to kick against the pricks" (Acts 9:4). With heavenly care and compassion Jesus concerned himself with the offender, in this case, Saul of Tarsus. The Master explained, it shall be, hard for you, to continue to kick against my will. You will cause harm to yourself by so doing.

How could this not be the creator of the heavens and the earth? How could this not be he who had made man in his own image through the direction of his father? How could this not be the resurrected Son of the living God?

A Physical Description of Paul

Paul himself admits to having been "abnormally born" (1 Cor. 15:8). Perhaps suggesting some kind of deformity such as being crooked or hunch-backed, that tormented him. (2 Cor. 12:7). In *The History of the Contending of Saint Paul* his countenance is actually described as "ruddy with the ruddiness of the skin of the pomegranate" and *The Acts of Saint Peter* confirms that Paul had a bald and shining head, with red hair. As summarized by Barnes, Chrysostom records that Paul's stature was low, his body crooked and his head bald. Lucian, in his Philopatris, describes Paul as "corpore erat parvo (he was small), contracto (contracted), incurvo (crooked), tricubitali (of three cubits, or four feet six)", while Nicephorus claims that Paul was a little man, crooked, and almost bent like a bow, with a pale countenance, long and wrinkled, and a bald head. Pseudo-Chrysostom echoes Lucian's height of Paul, referring to him as "the man of three cubits" (From Wikipedia, the free encyclopedia).

The Contributions of the Apostle Paul

Perhaps more than any of the other apostles, as a missionary, Paul traveled farther and preached to more people of more nations. In Paul's writings, he provides the first written account of what it is to be a Christian and thus a description of Christian spirituality. His letters have been characterized as being the most influential books of the New Testament after the Gospels of Matthew and John.

"Paul's letters reveal a remarkable human being: dedicated, compassionate, emotional, sometimes harsh and angry, clever and quick-witted, supple in argumentation, and above all possessing a soaring, passionate commitment to God: Jesus Christ, and his own mission. Fortunately, after his death one of his followers collected some of the letters, edited them very slightly, and published them. They constitute one of history's most remarkable personal contributions to religious thought and practice" (From Wikipedia, the free encyclopedia).

The Goad or Prick

The Savior showed us his mercy, compassion and perfect love when instead of condemning Saul of Tarsus, he said, "Saul, Saul, why persecutes me? It is hard for thee to kick against the pricks" (Acts 26:14).

The goad or *prick* as it was called in the time of Jesus, was a traditional implement used to spur or guide livestock, usually oxen, which are pulling a plough or a cart. The goad or prick is a long stick made with a sharpened metal point. When an unruly or obstinate ox would refuse to move forward, the man walking beside the ox would then prod him with the goad and if the ox would kick against the goad, he would drive it even deeper into his flesh. The goad or prick has been in use since Old Testament times. Shamgar son of Anath killed six hundred Philistines with an ox goad. (See, Judges 3:31).

The Apostle Paul
and Joan of Arc

When Paul was baptized he would have

been required to go through the repentance process causing him to ask forgiveness of all he had inflicted harm or damage to. Perhaps more importantly, someone with a forgiving heart (probably Ananias) would have had to perform the ordinance of baptism for Paul. (Acts 22:16). Paul's story reminds me of the life of Joan of Arc.

On 23 May 1430, she was captured at Compiègne by the Burgundian faction, which was allied with the English. She was later handed over to the English and put on trial by the pro-English Bishop of Beauvais Pierre Cauchon on a variety of charges. After Cauchon declared her guilty she was burned at the stake on 30 May 1431, dying at about nineteen years of age. Twenty-five years later, on July 7, 1456, an inquisitorial court authorized by Pope Callixtus III examined the trial, debunked the charges against her, pronounced her innocent, and declared her a martyr. Today Joan of Arc is a patron saint of France. (From Wikipedia, the free encyclopedia). Thus Joan of Arc was forgiven. It is nice to know that the idea of forgiveness has been around and practiced for a very long time.

The Importance of "Truth"

Now let us consider the word, "truth." What does this word mean? As it is used here, I believe the word "truth" refers directly to Jesus Christ. Jesus is the "light of truth." (See Psalms 43:3). Christ is, "the light shining in the darkness and the darkness comprehendeth it not" (John 1:5). Jesus is "the light of the world" (John 8:12).

Spiritually speaking, "light is truth and truth is light." The two are synonymous. Therefore, when a man has truth, he has Jesus Christ in his life. I believe Solomon is telling us to bind mercy, which enables a man to forgive and Jesus Christ who is light and truth, about our heart. Jesus will then assure our hearts that "forgiving" another is the right thing to do.

Trusting God

The following words leap off the page for me each time I read them. They are, "Trust in the Lord with all thine heart; and lean not unto thine own understanding. In all thy ways acknowledge him, and he shall direct thy paths" (Proverbs 3:5-6).

There is a difference between loving someone and trusting them. God loves all his children because he is their father. Trust however, is something that must be earned. I suggest that just as God will not forgive those who do not forgive others, so it is that God will not be able to trust those who do not first trust him.

However, when one does trust God, that act becomes a great enabler. That act of trusting God will enable the one who does trust God, to forgive those who trespass against him, even his enemies. And that is where you want to arrive in this life because until you forgive those who have offended or trespassed against you, God will not forgive you. But how must one trust God?

The author of Proverbs has spelled it out for us. "Trust in the Lord with all thine heart" (Proverbs 3:5). And so we see the pattern of how to interact with God continues. God wants all of our heart in everything we do with him. Jesus gave us the first great commandment: "Thou shalt love the Lord thy God with *all* thy heart, and with *all* thy soul, and with *all* thy mind" (Mt. 22:37). To be able to trust God is greater than being able to love God, because trust must be earned. One does not just trust someone because he is driven by faith. Just as a parent may love his or her children because their children are their own, it is not as easy to trust children without first proving them.

You may have heard that men and women are placed on the earth to be tested by God. That is true. This is the time to prove to God, that you can be trusted. The way to speed up that process is for a man or a woman to first trust God.

One way to do that is to understand that God, and not man, is in control of everything. God has made everything including you and me. John the Beloved has said, referring to the Son of God: "All things were made by him and without him was not anything made that was made" (John 1:3). To understand God, man would do well to study, search and ponder his words.

The word of God can be found in the scriptures. For instance, the verses we began with here are found in the third chapter of Proverbs. That scripture does not just say, "Trust in the Lord with all thine heart and lean not unto thine own understanding." It continues to say:

"In all thy ways acknowledge him and he shall direct thy paths" (Proverbs 3:5-6).

Concerning the Lord's promise to direct our paths let me assure you that that promise of the Son of God to all of mankind is true and faithful. When we acknowledge the hand of God in our lives and give all the honor and glory to God for our successes, God will absolutely direct our paths as he desires.

For most of us, it seems to take years to realize that God is always there, directing us if we do what he asks of us. Far beyond directing our paths, angels are ever there protecting those who acknowledge God. For example, when I was serving in the Chaplain corps in Cam Rahn Bay, Vietnam, there was not one, but several incidents that assured me this was true.

I was given permission by the commanding chaplain to travel six separate times to the Air Force barracks about five miles away in an Army jeep. I traveled after work hours in the evening alone and with no weapon. I would be doing the Lord's work. Therefore, I would be on the Lord's errand. I managed to make the six consecutive trips without incident and without harm.

However, it was but a few weeks later when a series of events happened that let me know I had been protected on each journey. A short time later, I was walking through our compound one afternoon and I suddenly heard the report of outgoing fire from an M16. Although the Religious Retreat Center in which I served was sitting in a war zone, we had not had any incident until then. I made my way over to the guard tower to talk to the soldier who fired the shots towards the open field next to our compound. He told me that he had spotted a sapper and he had just called in a Cobra gunship.

Sappers burrow under the ground digging tunnels to be able to throw a satchel charge of TNT into the barracks of sleeping soldiers. When the Cobra gunship arrived it quickly began to move up into the sky and then come down in a dive firing its mini Gatling gun at the enemy. I later learned from a Cobra gunship pilot that the gun fired 3,000 rounds per minute and that one pass in his gunship would cover an area the size of one football field so that nothing above ground could survive. The open field adjacent our compound was about the size of two football fields. One gunship was unable to get the job done, so another was called in.

If you ever want to hear the sound of the destroying angel, try standing on the ground below two Cobra gunships simultaneously diving and firing at the enemy. There is no other sound like that on earth that I had ever heard before or since!

When the job was done the two war birds made their way back to their base like two harmless although loud butterflies. The Viet Cong sapper's body was left draped over

Concertina wire in front of the field where he was killed, to intimidate the enemy.

We were not even issued weapons until this incident occurred. In just a few more days, I was traveling to the Air Force check out gate to take our local Vietnamese workers back to their village homes. Just as I stopped at the gate an enemy rocket came in quickly and landed less than one hundred yards from us on an Air Force runway. You should have seen how fast the local workers scrambled under the pick-up truck we traveled in for protection. I found myself scrambling with them. It is pretty hard to mistake the sound of an incoming rocket. Just a few days after this event, while getting ready for sleep one night and listening to music from a reel-to-reel tape recorder with headphones, I was suddenly knocked out of bed by an explosion of jet fuel more than three miles down our peninsula. The enemy had managed to blow up a very large supply of Air Force jet fuel.

I scrambled to get dressed and get outside. There was a flame in the sky about forty or fifty feet in the air and the flame did not die for three or more days. Just as we all got down on our tummies like scared jackrabbits, a secondary explosion blew a wave of energy over our heads.

These three events took place in succession and I am certain I was protected each time. Furthermore, I am certain I was protected when I traveled alone at night six times to do the

Lord's work with no weapon before these events occurred.

If three witnesses is not enough to convince you that God does direct the paths of those who acknowledge his hand in all things, here is one more incident.

When I was transferred to Da Nang to finish my tour of duty in country, I was asked to pull guard duty one night. It was monsoon season, so the ground was muddy. I was issued an M16 and one clip of ammunition. I was assigned a guard tower and would be on duty there from sundown to sunup. While on guard duty, two enemy rockets came in and landed next to the 50-caliber machine gun guard post. The rockets landed less than 100 yards from me.

The rockets landed in the mud and neither one exploded. How was that possible? Perhaps one would have not exploded, but to have two rockets not explode?

I am absolutely certain that the Lord was protecting me on that evening as well. The following day I enjoyed the Bob Hope show on a rainy day. But the night before, God's angels were not sleeping.

We Must Be Humble to Be Able to Forgive

Then certainly and almost over-whelmingly, the Lord is teaching us to be humble when he has his prophet Solomon write, "Be not wise in thine own eyes: fear the Lord and depart from evil. It shall be health to thy navel, and marrow to thy bones" (Proverbs 3:7-8).

In other words, trust God and not yourself. Do not think you know more than God about anything, because you do not.

Furthermore, we learn to give the credit for every good thing that happens in our life to God. Don't think you have accomplished anything by yourself. God is at the helm and not you. The sooner you acknowledge the fact that God is in control of all things and give all the honor and glory to God, the sooner you will be on the path that will lead you to peace and happiness. In so doing you will find success in this life, and eternal life and eternal happiness in the world to come.

Honoring the Lord
By Tithing

Solomon continues to teach us wisdom when he instructs us to: "Honour the Lord with thy substance, and with the first fruits of all thine increase: So shall thy barns be filled with plenty, and thy presses shall burst out with new wine" (Proverbs 3:9-10).

God doesn't need our money, our real estate or any of our possessions. He already owns everything. He has made everything.

All men were made in the image of God. All of mankind are children of God, and as such, men should respect their creator. One way to begin doing that is by honoring the Lord with our substance. We who have been given much should remember from whence our blessings come. You can't take it with you when you die. You have to leave it all behind. We are only the caretakers of that which we may have while we are alive.

Accepting Correction

Next, the Lord's messenger teaches us a great principle which will be a guide for you to know just when you will be on your way to becoming able to "forgive."

Solomon has written, "My son, despise not the chastening of the Lord; neither be weary of his correction: For whom the Lord loveth he correcteth; even as a father the son in whom he delighteth" (Proverbs 3:11-12).

When was the last time you were corrected by someone? How did you react? Did you accept the correction given to you thankfully? Did you feel that you were being picked on and resent being corrected?

When you are able to accept correction happily and even be thankful for it-you will be on your way to being able to forgive another.

Help People, Lift People, Love One Another

Jesus spent his mortal ministry teaching us to help one another, to lift one another, to love one another as he has loved us. That is exactly what Solomon is teaching us when he says, "Withhold not good from them to whom it is due, when it is in the power of thine hand to do it.

Say not unto thy neighbor, Go, and come again, and to morrow I will give; when thou hast it by thee" (Proverbs 3:27-28).

I believe that anything the Savior included in his majestic "Sermon on the Mount" is worth our serious attention. These words stand by themselves in the fifth chapter of Matthew, "Give to him that asketh thee, and from him that would borrow of thee turn not thou away" (Matthew 5:42).

Helping our neighbors by serving them and giving love to them when needed will help us to forgive them.

Wisdom

The Lord's servant, Solomon, was considered the wisest person on earth during his day. It is refreshing and worth our attention therefore, when he addresses the importance of obtaining wisdom and understanding in this life.

He has written, "Happy is the man that findeth wisdom, and the man that getteth understanding. For the merchandise of it is better than the merchandise of silver, and the gain thereof than fine gold" (Proverbs 3:13-14).

The Lord's prophet teacher continues instructing us on the virtues of wisdom and understanding. He writes, "She is more precious than rubies: and all the things thou canst desire are not to be compared unto her. Length of days is in her right hand; and in her left hand riches and honour" (Proverbs 3:15-16).

"The Lord by wisdom hath founded the earth; by understanding hath he established the heavens` (Proverbs 3:19). "By his knowledge the depths are broken up, and the clouds drop down the dew. My son, let not them depart from thine eyes: keep sound wisdom and discretion: So shall they be life unto thy soul, and grace to thy neck" (Proverbs 3: 20-22). *Then shalt thou walk in thy way safely, and thy foot shall not stumble" (Proverbs 3: 23).*

What a promise it is to know it is possible to go through your life and not stumble! Such is the promise to all if we can manage to obtain wisdom and understanding.

Understanding

Have you considered this? That which God may wish for us to understand is not just why we do what we do, but why others do what they do. For example, there will always be someone out there who will offend you by that which they say or do or do not do that you may wish they did. But have you ever taken the time to ask the question, why did they behave that way?

Imagine the new and different person you will be when you finally begin to understand the things of God? We read from the scripture, "There is a spirit in man and the inspiration of the Almighty giveth them understanding" (Job 32:8).

That is true. God created your spirit self, before he made the physical part of you that you can see with your eyes. The Holy Ghost is also real. The Holy Ghost can inspire men to understand the things of God. The spirit of the Lord or the Holy Ghost communicates to man by speaking to the spirit within man and not man's physical self.

I have always been aware of the poor. However, until I spent over a year trying to write this book, I did not realize that caring for the poor is absolutely necessary if we hope to have God forgive us for the sins we have committed. That understanding came because I have prayed to understand, and because I have followed what the Prophet Solomon outlined in the third chapter of Proverbs, which you have just read.

We Cannot Be Forgiven By God If We Fail to Help the Poor

Although it is not written in stone that we must first care for the poor in order for God to forgive us of our sins, it is certainly inferred in the scriptures.

The idea of helping or caring for those around us is not a new one. Jesus gave us the second great commandment during his mortal ministry wherein he said, "Thou shalt love thy neighbor as thyself" (Matthew 22:39). However, the Savior of the world was careful to mention six specific possibilities when he spoke of helping, caring for, loving and serving the poor within the parable of The Sheep and the Goats found in the twenty-fifth chapter of Matthew, verses 31-46).

I Was An Hungered and Ye Gave Me Meat

One of my neighbors just told this story about a fishing adventure he recently experienced. He explained that while he was fishing at his favorite spot he decided to walk further up the river to find another place he had never fished before. He soon discovered a homeless man living in a tent. When the man saw the fish he had caught he asked, "can you give the next fish you catch to me, I haven't eaten in two days?" My neighbor then invited this man to join him for a nice chicken dinner. He drove the man in his convertible to a place to eat. He said the homeless man insisted on bringing his ruck sack containing all he possessed with him. He did not want to leave it behind.

When was the last time you provided food for someone who had not enjoyed a good meal in awhile?

Thirsty and Ye Gave Me Drink

Why does Jesus mention giving drink to the thirsty? Could it be that water is a basic necessity to sustaining life? Could it be that water makes up 70 percent of the human body and coincidentally more than 70 percent of the earth is covered in water. (From NASA, fact sheet, 04-16-07).

Unless you have been in a place where the temperature is 122 degrees outside, you probably do not yet know how important it is to have water nearby to drink. When I was visiting friends in Scottsdale, Arizona in 1985 the temperature in Phoenix was 122 degrees. The radio disk jockey came on the air and warned that if you were out driving you should have a drink of water every 20 minutes.

"Humans need an average of two quarts of water a day. Water is in our blood, our cells, our tissues and body fluids. Water allows nutrients to circulate throughout the body and allows the body to filter out waste and poisons. Water also allows the body to regulate its temperature. Without water our bodies become dehydrated. Humans can survive for about three days without water" (From quest.nasa.gov).

A married couple I know returns to Kenya each spring to dig wells so that the natives who live there will have water in their villages to drink and not have to walk for miles to obtain it.

I Was A Stranger and You Took Me In

Once while I lived in Arizona a stranger came to my front door. He told me that his car had broken down and he needed a place to spend the night. I did not know this young man from Adam. I had never seen him before and he had never before seen me. He said he would be gone early in the morning. I invited him to sleep in an empty bedroom. When I awoke he was gone and I have not seen him again. Why did I let this stranger into my home and give him a place to spend the night? I did so because it felt right at the time. I felt impressed that he needed help and if I helped him all would be well. Helping others requires us to use our common sense but we should also follow God's promptings to us.

There is a scripture I like that speaks to us about so living. It reads, "Be not forgetful to entertain strangers for thereby some have entertained angels unawares" (Hebrews 13:2).

Naked and Ye Clothed Me

During his mortal ministry the Savior of the world did not own a fancy and expensive garment made of purple silk and spun gold. From all reports, Jesus wore a simple white robe and sandals. Following his crucifixion the soldiers cast lots to acquire what remained of his earthly possessions.

There are some who own closets filled with fine clothes and dozens of pairs of shoes. Yet the poor often get by with the clothes on their backs and no shoes at all. I don't believe the Lord was talking about those who are literally "naked" in this parable. I believe we are being invited to clothe those who are wearing rags or those who own but one or two outfits to wear in this life.

When was the last time you helped to clothe the less fortunate? When was the last time you gave an extra pair of trousers, skirt, dress, blouse, warm coat or shoes to someone less fortunate than you?

I Was Sick and Ye Visited Me

It is one thing to visit the sick but it is quite another to offer them something that only you can give them. For example, some have the gift to make homemade chicken soup. A child can perhaps draw a drawing with crayons or colored pencils. Some have the gift of music and they can sing songs. Others may just sit and tell stories or just be still and listen and hold a sick person's hand. To show up for a visit is great but if we do a little extra such as picking some wild flowers or making something with our hands, that can only add to our visit. Jesus was able to heal the sick. The apostle Peter once said to a man sitting outside the temple and asking for alms, "Silver and gold have I none, but such as I have, I freely give, in the name of Jesus Christ of Nazareth, rise up and walk" (Acts 3:6).

I Was in Prison and Ye Came Unto Me

When was the last time you visited

someone in prison? Have you ever done this even once in your life? For me, the last time I did this was while I was serving in the Army in Southeast Asia. While serving in DaNang, Vietnam, I visited prisoners in the Long Bin Jail. There were only two incarcerated there at the time.

On January 03, 1968, Johnny Cash visited Folsom Prison to perform a concert for the inmates incarcerated there. He later did a concert at San Quentin Prison and one of the inmates who heard him sing was Meryl Haggard. Haggard became a world famous country singer and songwriter and one wonders if that would have ever happened, if he was not inspired, by seeing Johnny Cash perform his songs for him while he was a prisoner. These acts of service may have touched hundreds of other lives and helped the inmates who heard Cash perform his songs to change their lives around. One may never know how many others will benefit from our small acts of kindness and service to others.

In the motion picture, "Sullivan's Travels" the prisoners were allowed to attend a local church house where they were privileged to watch a motion picture show of cartoons which had them all escaping from their own reality of serving many years as prisoners.

Bringing joy, happiness, laughter and entertainment to the downtrodden may do more good than we will ever know.

Caring For Others and Serving Them Should Continue Throughout Our Lives

Caring for those around us is not a one-time act. We should be constantly mindful of those around us and most especially, "the poor" as to the material things of this world. Our caring for and loving others should be done in some small way every day.

Some have referred to this as service to others, loving our neighbors, succoring the sick, helping the downtrodden, or lifting up the needy. We should be doing all of these things. If calling this "service to others" helps one to understand the principle of loving our neighbors as we love ourselves then that is a good thing.

If everyone in the world would perform one small act of kindness every day, it would not be long until the ripple effect of those acts of caring would change the world for the better in a very short time.

To illustrate, by throwing a large rock into the shallow part of a lake, one can notice the ripples of water moving ever outward. It is the same when we perform small acts of kindness to others. Something as simple as a friendly greeting, a pat on the back, a clasp of hands, a sincere compliment such as, "you look nice" can have a dramatic effect on the one who receives such interaction from another.

For example, Jesus said, from this same parable of the Sheep and the Goats, "For inasmuch as ye have done it unto one of the least of these my brethren, ye have done it unto me" (Matthew 25:40). When I read or hear those words I always think of those I have seen with signs on the side of the roads of life asking for help. When I look into their eyes I often wonder if I am looking at an angel waiting to see if I recognize them and will be willing to help them.

Next time you see someone holding up a sign on the side of the road asking for help, I wonder if you will be able to look into their eyes and see the eyes of an angel or even the eyes of our beloved Savior looking back at you.

Remember, Jesus said, "For inasmuch as ye have done it unto one of the least of these my brethren, ye have done it unto me" (Matthew 25:40).

The Rich Man and Lazarus

I like the story of the rich man and Lazarus. Please observe what happens when each man leaves this life: "There was a certain rich man, which was clothed in purple and fine linen, and fared sumptuously every day; And there was a certain beggar named Lazarus, which was laid at his gate, full of sores, And desiring to be fed with the crumbs which fell from the rich man's table: moreover the dogs came and licked his sores. And it came to pass, that the beggar died and was carried by the angels into Abraham's bosom: the rich man also died, and was buried; And in hell he lift up his eyes, being in torment, and seeth Abraham afar off, and Lazarus in his bosom. And he cried and said, Father Abraham, have mercy on me, and send Lazarus, that he might dip the tip of his finger in water, and cool my tongue for I am tormented in this flame.

But Abraham said, Son, remember that thou in thy lifetime received thy good things, and likewise Lazarus evil things, but now he is comforted, and thou art tormented. And beside all this, between us and you there is a great gulf fixed, so that they which would pass from hence to you cannot; neither can they pass to us, that would come from thence.

Then he said, I pray thee therefore, father, that thou wouldest send him to my father's house. For I have five brethren; that he may testify unto them, lest they also come into this place of torment. Abraham saith unto him, They have Moses and the prophets; let them hear them. And he said, Nay, father Abraham: but if one went unto them from the dead, they will repent. And he said unto him, If they hear not Moses and the prophets, neither will they be persuaded, though one rose from the dead" (Luke 16:19-31).

Therefore, equally important to forgiving those who trespass against us in our quest to have our sins forgiven by God is the absolute necessity for all of God's children to care for the poor.

Someone has said, "Whoever has the most toys when he dies wins." At first hearing, that sounds pretty convincing and many people seem to buy into this little quip. But the truth is, that little saying turns out to be a lie. Although they tried to take it with them, the Egyptians left all of their material wealth behind when they died. Try as they may, the Egyptians could not take their earthly treasures with them.

Someone else has said, "I ain't never seen a hearse with a luggage rack." Jesus taught, "Lay not up for yourselves treasures on earth, where moth and rust dost corrupt, but lay up for yourselves treasures in heaven where neither moth nor rust doth corrupt" (Matthew 6:19-20).

When the Son of God walked the earth during his mortal ministry, he had no material possessions. He wore only a robe and sandals. He certainly owned no mansion on a hill or on some exotic island. He had no chauffeur with a private limousine. He walked to his destination or took someone else's small sailing vessel.

When the Savior of the world spent 40 days and nights in the desert fasting, he almost certainly slept on the ground. Jesus said, "The foxes have holes and the birds of the air have nests; but the Son of man hath not where to lay his head" (Matthew 8:20).

He who has made the universe has promised us, "In my Father's house are many mansions: if it were not so I would have told you. I go to prepare a place for you" (John 14:2). The Son of man spent his ministry on earth teaching all men by his example, to care for others and most especially, to care for the poor.

To the rich young ruler who asked the

Lord, "Good Master, what good thing shall I do, that I may have eternal life? Jesus replied by saying, if thou wilt enter into life, keep the commandments. He saith unto him, Which? Jesus said, "Thou shalt do no murder, Thou shalt not commit adultery, Thou shalt not steal, Thou shalt not bear false witness. Honour thy father and thy mother: and, Thou shalt love thy neighbor as thyself. The young man saith unto him, All these things have I kept from my youth, what lack I yet" (Matthew 19:16-20)?

"Jesus said unto him, If thou wilt be perfect, go and sell that thou hast, and give to the poor, and thou shalt have treasure in heaven: and come and follow me" (Matthew 19:21; Mark 10:21; Luke 18:22).

"But when the young man heard that saying he went away sorrowful: for he had great possessions. Then said Jesus unto his disciples, Verily, I say unto you, That a rich man shall hardly enter into the kingdom of heaven. And again I say unto you, it is easier for a camel to go through the eye of a needle, than for a rich man to enter into the kingdom of God" (Matthew 19:16-24).

How to Forgive Another

You cannot forgive your neighbor if you hate him. That would be an oxymoron. You don't want to be an ox and you don't want to be a moron. I have heard some say, "I don't hate my neighbor but I don't like him. Truth be told, I can't stand him. I don't trust him because of what

I have seen him do to others."

Although it may not be possible to avoid seeing how your neighbors deal with others, it is possible for you to learn not to judge your neighbor. Jesus has given us one way to do this. The Son of God said, "Father forgive them; for they know not what they do" (Luke 23:34).

Another way to stop judging our neighbors in order that we might be able to forgive them is to realize that judging another is not our job. For it is written, "Vengeance is mine: I will repay, saith the Lord" (Romans 12:19). All men should learn to say, "Forgiveness is mine and I will learn to do that."

Another way to learn to forgive is to stop focusing on the other fella's faults and begin to, look for the good things they do. Virtually everyone does some good things. Virtually everyone bears some good fruit.

Yet another way to learn to forgive another is to allow people to make mistakes. If you do not allow others to make mistakes, in essence, you are saying to the world, "I am perfect." There is only one perfect man who has walked the earth and that is Jesus Christ. If you truly believe you do not make mistakes, it is time for you to take a humility pill and let gravity bring you back down to earth with the rest of us mere mortals.

One of my favorite ways to effect a positive change in anyone's life is to develop a genuine sense of humor. By this I do not mean being able to laugh at another person's jokes or another person's weaknesses. I mean you must begin to start acknowledging your own shortcomings. You will even want to make fun of your weaknesses in public from time to time thereby admitting to the world that you are human after all.

Finally, if you hope to be a success at forgiving others, let gratitude be a permanent part of your true character. I believe a grateful heart is a forgiving heart. When was the last time you said, "thank you" and truly meant it? If you hope to get into the "forgiving business" begin by saying, "thank you" many times every day. Be grateful for everything you have, even the very air you breathe. We should begin each day with prayer and end each day thankful that we have been given another day to live. We should not just be praying for the things we need, but we should be saying our thanks for the things we already have and certainly for our prayers that have been answered.

We Must Forgive All Who Trespass Against Us

One of the most powerful modern day accounts of one man forgiving others for their trespasses against him is that of Captain Louis Zamperini. I don't believe it is possible to read his story without coming away better for having done so.

Captain Louis Zamperini

Louis Zamperini was an Olympic Athlete, a World War II prisoner of war and war hero. But all of that did not just happen by accident.

When the family moved to Torrance California in the early 1930's Zamperini only spoke Italian and he quickly became the person of choice for bullies to taunt and beat up. He would take the beatings without uttering a word and without ever breaking down to cry. As he grew older, he taught himself to box. On one momentous day when the head bully came to face Zamperini down, he dodged the first blow of the bully then he hauled off and slugged him hard enough; that he was never bothered by him or other bullies again.

Louis Zamperini had an indomitable spirit. He was a man who would not quit or give up, no matter what. That spirit of seeing all things to the end did not just happen by itself. Zamperini's older brother, Pete, saw potential greatness in him when he was just a teenager. He needed someone who would guide him.

As a young boy, he spent most of his time being chased by, and running away from, the police. But Pete figured out back then that the reason his brother was constantly getting into trouble was because he craved attention. He would soon be able to get the attention he craved by participating in sports.

Pete was always there for his younger brother, constantly encouraging him and supporting him and believing in him with positive words like: "If you can take it, you can make it." Those very words enabled Zamperini to qualify for the 1936 Olympic games.

Plane Crash into the Pacific Ocean

In 1943 as World War II was raging, the then Captain Zamparini, was called to undertake a rescue mission in the South Pacific. Because of engine failure, his plane crashed into the vast expanse of the Pacific Ocean.

Zamperini survived 47 days being lost at sea, eluding hungry sharks; the strafing of a Japanese bomber; sustaining life only by capturing rain water, and eating raw fish, an Albatross and a Turpin. When the tiny raft finally did reach the Solomon Islands, Zamperini and one more of the three airmen who survived the plane crash; were immediately captured by the Japanese Navy. Now Zamperini and his comrade would face more than two years of imprisonment as a POW from his capture in 1943 until the end of the war.

Two Years of Being a Prisoner of War

Captain Zamperini was singled out as an example: by the man in charge of the POW's at the time. Sergeant Watanabe, "the Bird," became his persecutor and tormentor. He was beaten with a bamboo cane and hit in the face with Watanabe's belt. This torture and more went on not for two days or two weeks, but for two years, and Zamperini did not break. Sergeant Watanabe would later say of this man, "Six hundred prisoner, Zamperini number one."

The End of World War II

When the war ended, Zamperini returned home to the arms of his loving family. But, having survived more than two years as a tortured POW, the war for him was still not over. He swore revenge for the years of abuse and torture he suffered from the hands of Sergeant Watanabe, "the Bird."

As noted, The "Bird," was Zamperini's greatest tormentor for the time he was a POW. When he returned home after the war, he escaped his POW nightmares, of more than two years of torture by becoming periodically drunk for years. He would awake in a cold sweat from dreaming of strangling "the Bird" to death with his bare hands.

His hatred and anger for Sergeant Watanabe and his drinking nearly caused his marriage to end in divorce until his wife attended a nearby crusade and was converted to Christianity. She told her husband about her conversion and invited him to the crusade but he refused. His wife continued to invite him and he finally accepted on the condition that he leave before the invitation to respond began.

However, when the invitation came, Zamperini's heart was struck. It could have been the memory of his mother reading the Bible to him as a boy that caused his heart to begin to soften. Then he recalled a long forgotten promise he made to God when he was lost in the vast expanse of the Pacific Ocean, adrift for 47 days, with one other survivor (a third had already succumbed). Louis Zamperini promised God, "If you will save me, I will serve you for the rest of my life." He soon found himself on his knees under the crusade tent, his heart now broken, now willing to submit himself to God's will.

Zamperini's conversion to Christ had begun. The bitterness, and the anger he had held for "the Bird" had now gone. His quest to murder his tormentor left him. He returned home, emptied the bottles of booze stored in his house, trashed other unsavory materials, and began his life anew. His greatest victory began when he remembered the promise he made to God one night, while stranded on a raft in the vast expanse of the Pacific Ocean, "If you will save me, I will serve you for the rest of my life."

Jesus is always standing at our door knocking. God waits on man to use his agency. God waits on man to choose to let God into his life. God waits on man to hear his voice and then open the door to his own heart. God has promised all men, if they will draw near unto him, He will then draw near unto them. But it is left up to men to take the first step.

Zamperini Returns to Japan to Forgive Those Who Tortured Him

So powerful was the message of forgiveness that Captain Zamperini shared with the prison guards whom he faced during his visit to the place he was a POW for more than two years, that some of them became Christians. Although he was not able to face the man who tortured him by hitting him in the face with his belt and beating him with a bamboo cane, Zamperini did forgive this man also. *This is how the gospel of Jesus Christ works. It is a wonderful thing to see. (The preceding material regarding Lois Zamperini from, Wikipedia, the free encyclopedia and Laura Hillenbrand's fine book, "Unbroken").*

Love Precedes Forgiveness
Forgiveness Conquers Hate

You cannot talk about forgiveness without talking about love, and not love as the world knows it. The love the world knows fades with time. Christ's love grows with use and with time. The more you love the way Christ desires, the more motivation and capacity to love Christ's way, grows inside us.

One might argue that the Watanabe's or "Birds" of the world, need to be punished. Such people (the tormentors, the people who inflict great harm, even torturing others) need to suffer for their crimes and they need to suffer big. One could continue to argue, "I am justified because look how many there are in agreement with me!"

The acquiescence of many does not satisfy justice. In addition, you as an individual are not qualified to make that judgment call. When all men take their respective turns and stand to be judged before God, it will be Christ who judges man by and through those he has called, chosen, ordained and set apart to judge the twelve tribes of the earth. Our job is not to judge men but to forgive all men of their offenses and to ask forgiveness of all we have offended. No, we cannot forget completely, but we can forgive.

When Jesus hung on the cross, just before he declared, "It is finished," (Father thy will is finished, emphasis added) and gave up the ghost, the Lord made a final plea for all of his persecutors. For all who had tormented and tortured and dishonored him, as previously noted, Jesus pled: "Father forgive them, for they know not what they do" (Luke 23:34). Those words did not specify, "Father forgive these only and not those." The words of Jesus were all encompassing. The inference was, "Father forgive all who have not loved me and have not believed that I am the Son of God, for they know not what they do" Can we do any less?

The Vital Role of the Atonement in Allowing Us to Forgive

An ex-husband abused the daughter of his former wife. How does one forgive such an act? I don't believe this is possible without the atonement of Jesus Christ. The Savior of the world has paid the price for all sin. We cannot atone for anyone's transgressions or sins but the Savior already has. It is our job to accept the Lord's atoning sacrifice and put it into action in our lives.

One of the surest ways to do this is by forgiving others for their transgressions against us. When we forgive another for their offenses toward us we are accessing the infinite atonement of Jesus Christ. By doing so, we are allowing the atonement of Jesus Christ to make up the difference for what we cannot do ourselves. I do not believe it would be possible for anyone to forgive another if the atonement of Jesus Christ was not already in place.

The fullness of the gospel of Jesus Christ centers on the infinite atonement of Jesus Christ because without it, all would be lost. Since all men and women are imperfect, without the atonement, no one could be saved in the kingdom of God.

How Often Must We Forgive Another Their Trespasses?

Get ready to forgive the same people over and over again because human beings are not perfect and all men and women will continue to make mistakes just as you will.

One southern gentleman said to me: "This here gospel of yours might be easy to understand but it sure enough ain't easy to live." "You are correct," I said. "I commend you for your astute observation. Upon first look, the gospel does seem hard to live. And by the way, it is the Lord's gospel and not mine.

But as for the gospel being hard to live, it really is not. That which makes the gospel seem hard to live is just the human side of us, wanting to maintain control of our own lives.

I inquired of him, "Would you care to give me a for instance as to why the gospel seems hard for you to live?" "I sure can. How about this here fella that cheated me out of all this land he sold me? This is land that never did even exist.

You mean to tell me, I'm supposed to forgive him?" I answered. "Yes. We are supposed to forgive all offenses." "You don't say." "I do say. That is, Jesus said it, not me."

For example, Peter was the chief apostle who was at the head of the twelve apostles in seniority when Jesus was on the earth. Peter came to Jesus one day and asked an interesting question: "Then came Peter to him, and said, Lord, how oft shall my brother sin against me, and I forgive him? Til seven times? Jesus saith unto him, I say not unto thee , Until seven times: but, until seventy times seven." (Matthew 18:21-22).

My friend then said, "Let's see, 70 times 7 that adds up to 140. So that means if I can hold my breath for 140 offenses that on the one hundred and forty-first, I get to let that fella have what for?" Then he said, "No, I was just funnin' with ya."

Then I said, "That is good, because Jesus wasn't finished teaching Peter what he had in mind about this forgiveness business. Get yourself an earful of this, "Therefore is the kingdom of heaven likened unto a certain king, which would take account of his servants. And when he had begun to reckon, one was brought unto him, which owed him ten thousand talents.

But forasmuch as he had not to pay; his lord commanded him to be sold, and his wife, and children, and all that he had, and payment to be made. The servant therefore fell down, and worshipped him, saying, Lord, have patience with me, and I will pay thee all.

Then the lord of that servant was moved with compassion, loosed him, and forgave him the debt. But the same servant went out, and found one of his fellow servants who owed him an hundred pence; and he laid hands on him, and took him by the throat, saying pay me that thou owest. And his fellow servant fell down at his feet, and besought him, saying, Have patience with me, and I will pay thee all. And he would not: but went and cast him into prison, till he should pay the debt. So when his fellow servants saw what was done, they were very sorry and came and told unto their lord all that was done.

Then his lord, after that he had called him said unto him, O thou wicked servant, I forgave thee all that debt, because thou desiredst me: Shouldest not thou also have had compassion on thy fellowservant, even as I had pity on thee? And his lord was wroth, and delivered him to the tormentors, till he should pay all that was due unto him. So likewise shall my heavenly Father do also unto you, if ye from your hearts forgive not every one his brother his trespasses" (Matthew 18:21-35).

My friend said, "Well, I'm not having any of that I can tell you, so I guess I'll forgive that fella. So what about this here rascal that cheated me out of all that money? It doesn't seem right to me that he should get off scot-free." "He won't get off scot-free," I assured my friend.

"Vengeance is mine: I will repay, saith the Lord" (Romans 12:19). "The Son of God is the judge of all the earth, and not man. Meanwhile, man should be in the forgiveness business. Let's leave the judgment business to God where it belongs." My friend said, "If I can be sure to not get any of that stuff you just read me about, that's good by me. I'll forgive the scoundrel and let God deal with him."

When one is able to forgive and ask forgiveness of others, that person is on his way to wisdom and understanding. That is the sacrifice God asks of all of us. This is the test all of us must pass. Those who are not able to forgive are prideful and the prideful are numbered with the wicked. Malachi prophesied long ago: "For behold, the day cometh, that shall burn as an oven, and all the proud; yea, and those that do wickedly, shall be as stubble; and the day that cometh shall burn them up, saith the Lord of Hosts, that it shall leave them neither root nor branch" (Malachi 4:1).

How Much Forgiving Must I Do Until My Character Changes?

Stretch Armstrong was a large, gel-filled action figure first introduced in 1976 by Kenner. He could be stretched out again and again to four or five feet and he always went back to his original shape of about 15 inches. (From Wikipedia, the free encyclopedia).

How many times will we have to forgive another until our character stretches out enough that it stays stretched out and becomes a little bit better each time we forgive? It will not be a mere seven times or even 70 times seven but it will go on until we finish our life on earth and then continue perhaps ad infinitum.

To say this, another way, forgiveness is not a one-time act. Forgiving another is something we must do multiple times and it will probably not end in this life.

Examples of Some Who Have Forgiven Others

Not long ago there was a newspaper headline that read something like this, "Man forgives drunk driver for killing his wife and two children." When the case went to trial the drunk driver stood up and said how sorry he was for his mistake and said he would spend the rest of his life seeking forgiveness for his mistake. The father of those who were killed then stood up and told the judge that he forgave the drunk driver and asked the judge to show mercy in his judgment of him since he would suffer enough for his mistake for the rest of his life.

A business owner friend shared this story with me: He left five or six of his vintage cars he would one day restore on someone else's property. He was invited to do so by the man renting the property. Although he left a note in the windshield of the cars saying, "If you have any questions, call this number," When he went to retrieve his cars they were gone and it appears they were taken inappropriately. The cars were worth several thousands of dollars. When I asked my friend how he would deal with this he said, "They were only cars."

Several years ago one of my ecclesiastical leaders was given a new assignment. With it would come added responsibilities and require him to stay close to the Lord. Besides already being an ecclesiastical leader he was also a successful business owner.

I had the occasion to ask him long ago, "What did you do to prepare yourself for your new assignment?" He said, "I had to forgive a lot of debt." I had just started my own business at the time and I thought I understood, the deeper meaning of my friend's answer.

Now that I have operated my own business for decades, I have also had the experience of forgiving many for not paying that which they owed. That experience has allowed me to more fully understand what my friend meant when he said, "I had to forgive a lot of debt.."

More than one person has forgiven those who committed horrible atrocities involving their families and loved ones during times of war. But for everyone who has forgiven such acts of horror, there are no doubt many more who still seek revenge for those who have imprisoned, tortured and even murdered their loved ones. To seek revenge; is the natural human instinct for all who have had harm inflicted upon them by another. The Law of Moses stated, "an eye for an eye and a tooth for a tooth." (Exodus 21:24). Those sentiments still remain in the hearts of many.

However, Jesus said, "Ye have heard that it has been said, "and eye for an eye and a tooth for a tooth, "But I say unto you, Love your enemies, bless them that curse you, do good to them that hate you, and pray for them which despitefully use you, and persecute you" (Matthew 5:44). Can you imagine how those words were received during the Savior's mortal ministry?

We must forgive everyone not just 70 times 7 but ad infinitum. Seeking revenge and wanting to get even is not our job. It never was our job.

Everyone Has Offended Someone Else Verbally

Every man and woman has offended at least someone with the spoken word. If you will not acknowledge that as the truth, then you are also saying you are a perfect man or woman. James made a sage observation when he said, "If any man offend not in word, the same is a perfect man, and able also to bridle the whole body" (James 3:2).

We know there are no perfect men or women, therefore we must conclude that James is correct, that is, everyone has offended someone with their words. Here are just a few examples: Anyone who has experienced a divorce will realize that beyond suing one's spouse for all that person may possess, the hurtful words that are spoken in anger can be equally painful unless there is a forgiving balm. James said, "But the tongue can no man tame; It is an unruly evil, full of deadly poison. Therewith bless we God, even the Father; and therewith curse we man, which are made after the similitude of God. Out of the same mouth proceedeth blessing and cursing, My brethren, these things ought not so to be" (James 3:8-10).

There may be more than just one of the following stories that resonates with the person on the wrong end of someone's hurtful words. Often, those hurtful words will be kept in someone's heart for decades. We must all get those bad feelings out of our hearts.

Two local leaders came over to a certain person's home and asked that person to contribute to an organization because they had done so in the past. The person in question said, "no" and the leaders said, "We'll have to put your name down in our book that you did not contribute."

Is this Nazi Germany? Are you members of the Gestapo writing people's names down in your black book and when you have enough offenses written down for them, will you then carry them off to a concentration camp? Please, please, please. Stop it! Think before you speak. This behavior, has in fact, driven people away from God, I have seen it. Please consider the consequences of your thoughtless behavior and your foolish words.

Does this rebuke sound a little strong? Perhaps it is not strong enough! If there is one person who is going about blindly thinking they are doing good but in fact are driving God's children away from Him, no words could be strong enough to put an end to that behavior. We want their names and your name written in the Lamb's book of life. You are moving in the wrong direction. Stop seeking faults many of which, probably never did exist. Let us look for the good in others!

What do you do when someone accuses you of doing something wrong up close and personal in front of others who are in the same room? To make matters worse, the accuser accuses you in front of two women and lets it be known that they are also wrong. You know you are not doing anything wrong but the accuser thinks you are. It is not enough for them to accuse you in public they also make their accusation in anger. But this is still not enough for the accuser, next they report you to higher authorities and now you are no longer able to do God's work. What should you do?

When you are first accused, this will be a good time to keep silent. When Jesus stood before Pilate to defend himself, Jesus answered Pilate not a word. "A soft answer turneth away wrath: but grievous words stir up anger" (Proverbs 15:1). The natural tendency of all men who are confronted and accused in anger is to

69

respond in anger. If you say anything at all to defend yourself even though there is no anger, there must surely be disappointment in the other person's behavior. Now it falls upon you to go to the offender and ask his forgiveness.

A certain man went up to the house of the Lord to serve and to worship. When he checked with the person in charge (someone who was new and unknown to him) he explained that he had been coming for many years. The new person then said, "You just do everything I tell you to do and we'll let you keep coming." The same man brought a friend with him to the same house of the Lord on another day but went to a different place to serve.

When the two men arrived to begin their service a lady who was new, now sitting at a desk, opened a desk drawer and took out a piece of paper with both of the men's names on it. She then called them both by name and welcomed them.

Then another gentleman appeared and welcomed the first man, who was long since, known by him, calling him by his name. When they were leaving a gentleman walked up to the first man and gave him a big hug and said, "It is so good to see you, I have missed you."

The man noticed this gentleman was limping and he asked, "Are you alright?" The other man said, "I have been away for awhile because of my injury, but I am getting better every day." The first man introduced his friend to this gentleman whereupon the man said, to his friend, "I just love this man." Which of these two men's behavior invites anyone to return to serve?

How Can I Know Whom It Is I May Have Offended?

"I had an experience awhile back that was most unusual. I began thinking about my days in high school. I remember very vividly, a young lady who had invited me to a Girl's Athletic Association dance. I already had an idea that she liked me because she made sandwiches for me, for a time, and gave them to me in front of the guys while we were walking out to our physical education class.

One day, she invited me to escort her to an upcoming Girl's Athletic Association dance. I did not take her to the dance and that was wrong of me. I thought I had a perfectly good reason back then but looking back, I was wrong, dead wrong.

Now, it was years later, I had graduated from college and was now serving others in the Maritime Provinces of Canada. When all of those old memories flooded into my mind, I was suddenly filled with remorse and sorrow, which I felt very deeply. I felt remorse for what I done back then.

I had a feeling come over me, which I had never before felt. I wanted to make that misgiving and mistake right with her and beg her forgiveness but of course, that was years ago by then, and I had no way of knowing how to find her now. I did not explain that the memory of my high school Spanish teacher who was also our high school advisor came into my mind.

That good lady whom I respected and loved for years, called my name out over the loud speaker one day while I was in physics class. This was during my senior year and it was my last class of the day. Needless to say, I was embarrassed to hear my name called out over the school's loudspeaker. I was asked to report to the principal's office immediately.

I must admit that I somehow knew right away what my Spanish teacher would be talking to me about was, this young lady. I knew I had not done anything else to deserve being called into the principal's office. I had never in all my years of high school been called into the principal's office. You should have seen my classmates look at me as I left physics class.

When I walked into the principal's office Mrs. ____was there to greet me. She invited me into her office and very gently explained that this was a good young lady, a popular young lady, a member of the Pep Club and the Girl's Athletic Association and that she had bought a brand new dress for the occasion, and I had done other than a gentlemanly thing by not escorting her to the big dance she was looking forward to so much.

I explained to Mrs. ____my reasons based on rumors, which I could not substantiate at the time. I was only 16 years old, but my age was no excuse. I was wrong. I was just too naïve then to know how much I had hurt this young lady. I began to get the idea however, when she had some of her male friends attempt to tip my car over while I was still in it with a friend at a Drive In movie.

As I have stated, these feelings came to me after I had graduated from college and towards the end of two years of serving others in Canada. All of those particular high school memories came flooding back into my mind. I decided to fast and pray and ask my Heavenly Father to forgive me for anyone and everyone I may have offended over the course of my lifetime.

I was sincere about that. I really meant it. If ever you want to know how you stand with all those around you, and all those you have ever known, just put yourself through that process and you will know, I assure you.

Not much time had passed when a letter or two started arriving The author of one of the letters I can remember, told me how I had deeply hurt the feelings of one member of their family by not allowing that person to do a certain thing. I truly had no intentions of hurting this person's feelings but I did.

When I found that out, I asked my Heavenly Father's forgiveness for that. I wrote a letter and apologized to that person also. Next, I began to find out whose feelings I had hurt of those right around me. I apologized to them and asked their forgiveness.

Finally, I began to be shown other shortcomings, and I endeavored to immediately repent of those. There is but one perfect man who has ever walked this earth, so it is very likely that you as well, may have hurt someone's feelings by something said or done, or left undone.

Please do not wait for those who have offended you to take the first step and ask for your forgiveness. You may wait many lifetimes for that to ever happen. You be the one to ask for forgiveness of those you have offended. Our Lord and Savior taught us, in what in my opinion, is perhaps the pinnacle of all human literature. That would be, his magnificent, Sermon on the Mount:

Therefore if thou bring thy gift to the altar, and there rememberest that thy brother hath ought against thee; Leave there thy gift before thy altar, and go thy way, first be reconciled to thy brother, and then come and offer thy gift" (Matthew 5:23-24). (Story, from My Greatest Love, Copyright © 2014 by Ronald H. Bartalini).

So if you want to know whom it is you may have offended, ask God with a sincere and humble prayer and you will know, I promise.

For those who are serious about God forgiving them of past mistakes, here are some additional thoughts to consider:

Warnings & Cautions

Being easily offended is not productive.

Holding a grudge is not productive.

Getting mad at God is not productive.

Thinking you know more than God is not productive.

Condemning others is not productive.

Not allowing others to make mistakes is not productive.

Not allowing yourself-to make mistakes is not productive.

Don't beat yourself up because you are not perfect.

Do not force your will upon others but allow others to be themselves.

Getting angry is not productive.

Trying to win an argument is not productive.

Belittling others is not productive.

Whining until you get your own way shows a lack of character and an absence of class.

Complaining is not productive.

Thinking only of yourself-is not productive.

Do not expect others to behave the way you think they should.

What to Do When Bad Things Happen

This story was told in church last Sunday. The lady telling the story explained, "I went to baby sit my little one month-old granddaughter last night. She fell asleep on my chest, we were cozy, and it was just the best experience for four hours. When my son and daughter in law returned home, my son asked, "Mom where is your car?" I said, "What do you mean?" He said, "Your car's not there." I said, "Are you joking?" He said, "No, your car is not there."

Well, to make a long story short, I got towed. I was furious. You do not want a Scotsman to get upset and I have Irish grandparents. My husband will testify you stand out of the way. I was so angry. How could this be? Here I am babysitting this one month-old baby. How could somebody tow my car?

My son felt so bad. We checked with our other children to see if they had come by and borrowed the car. I said, "I would hope it had been stolen because maybe I could get a new car but being towed would not be good." It turned out that I was towed. I called the towing company and asked, "do you have my car?" When they said they had it, I got madder and madder. When we drove over there my son would not let me out of the car because he knew I would really have to repent.

When I retrieved my car the attendant said, "Have a better night." I thought, "Do not look at him. Don't look at him." So I got in my car and I drove home. The first thing I said to my husband was, "You will never guess what happened to me, I am so mad! My car got towed. I was babysitting and my car got towed." He turned around and he said, "You can talk about it, or you can whine about it." So I took to heart what he said and I sat on my bed for about twenty minutes trying to calm myself down. And I really did have to calm myself down and pray and ask Heavenly Father to soften my heart. I prayed to be able to think kindly. The people who towed my car were just doing their job. There was a sign there I just didn't read it. I didn't read the sign.

So coming to church today held new meaning for me. Because my heart was really angry, I was really angry. So it is so wonderful to be able to come on a Sunday and partake of the Sacrament and be able to renew your covenants and to ask Heavenly Father to soften your heart. To ask Heavenly Father to bless you and to forgive you is a wonderful thing.

I am grateful for the atoning sacrifice of the Savior even on a simple case of getting your car towed and being upset with the man who towed your car. I am so grateful to come unto Christ and to be able to feel of his Spirit and to be able to know that I am a daughter of God. I know that Jesus is the Christ. I know that by him, great things happen. I know that the light of the world is the Savior and when we decide not to read our scriptures or we decide to skip prayer, we are cutting ourselves off from the Savior. And how important that is to have that communication with the Savior every day.

What Do You Do When You Are Publicly Accused?

What do you do if you are accused in a public meeting in front of everyone for not sharing your knowledge of God and our Savior properly? This is just so utterly wrong and preposterous that it is almost impossible to believe that anyone could be so insensitive to say such a thing! Please, never ever accuse anyone in a public meeting. Take them aside privately. But for you and only you, who may have done this, please never accuse anyone of anything ever again.

You have attacked another human being's personal witness of the Son of God and you have done it publicly, to his shame. You obviously have no idea how that could hurt another human being. Hello, Mr. Accuser: Don't you know that for anyone to be able to say, "Jesus is Lord" in any form or fashion and in any words requires the Holy Ghost to be present? (See 1 Corinthians 12:3).

One of my friends recently said to me, "The spirit of the Lord has been waking me up at three in the morning nudging me to go to the person who offended me." So I asked, "And how did that go." My friend said, "I haven't been able to do that yet." I then said, "This forgiveness business is not easy for any of us but it can be done." What will help is to pray and ask God to soften your heart and give you the desire to go to the person who offended you and ask his forgiveness for the unkind feelings you now have for him.

For Him Who Has Offended Another

Jesus said, "Not that which goeth into the mouth defileth a man: but that which cometh out of the mouth, that defileth a man" (Matthew 15:11). "Then answered Peter and said unto him, Declare unto us this parable. And Jesus said, Are ye also yet without understanding? Do not ye yet understand, that whatsoever entereth in at the mouth goeth into the belly, and is cast out into the draught? But those things which proceed out of the mouth come forth from the heart; and they defile the man. For out of the heart proceed evil thoughts, murders, adulteries, fornications, thefts, false witness, blasphemies: These are the things which defile a man: but to eat with unwashen hands defileth not a man" (Matthew 15:15-20).

When unkind or hurtful words leave our mouth, we cannot call them back. Now it becomes our responsibility to make that offense right with man and right with God. What you must do follows:

Ask Forgiveness of, All Those You Have Offended

Now we come to another piece of instruction Jesus gave us all in his Magnificent Sermon on the Mount. I would venture to say that few people understand it, and fewer people still, are out there, putting this counsel into practice. Here it is: "Therefore if thou bring thy gift to the altar, and there rememberest that thy brother hath ought against thee; Leave there thy gift before the altar, and go thy way; first be reconciled to thy brother, and then come and offer thy gift" (Matthew 5:23-24). I found one of the most memorable examples of putting this counsel into practice in one particular movie.

Sergeant Alvin York

According to the motion picture, "Sergeant York," Alvin York was a dirt-poor farmer who lived higher up in the hills of Tennessee where the soil was as poor as he was. More than anything, York wanted to own his own piece of bottomland that he might be able to grow more corn and other crops to have a better life. The motion picture, *Sergeant York* is in my opinion a perfect example of one man, Sergeant York, asking forgiveness of one of his neighbors for the ill feelings he held against him when it was his neighbor who should have been asking for his forgiveness.

When the film begins, York has not embraced religion with his family and most of his neighbors. He spends his private hours with two of his friends escaping to the border of Kentucky to carouse and imbibe in rotgut whiskey. It is discovered early on that Alvin is an expert marksman. While York is drunk on horseback, he still manages to shoot his initials perfectly into a large tree with his pistol, interrupting the local pastor who is trying to preach his sermon.

But it is not until York had his own encounter with God that his life changes. One night while he is returning home on his mule in a drunken stupor, carrying his rifle in a thunder and lightning storm and soaked from head to toe, he is struck by lightning. York and his mule are tossed to the ground. His rifle barrel is twisted and one of the mule's steel shoes is mangled but York survived.

This is York's version of seeing a light and hearing a voice from heaven. This is also his wake up call. York responds by picking himself up off the ground and immediately making his way to the nearby little church house where the meeting is now in session. He enters the building shaken, wet and tattered and makes his way to the congregation where he soon ends up on bended knee looking up to his pastor, and joining in singing the hymn, "Give Me That Old Time Religion."

From that moment on, York's life changed. He decided that he is now going to get some bottomland. York goes to the man he knows has some land for sale. He and the owner agree Alvin York will have 60 days to come up with all of the money or he will lose the small amount of money he had to secure his purchase and he will also lose his land. York is credited a small amount of money by the owner for a mule and what seems to be all the rest of his earthly possessions. But the landowner reminds York that he has only 60 days to obtain the balance owing. York responds by saying he also has 60 nights to come up with the money.

In the film, York is then seen sweating, toiling, and taking any available job for the most meager amount. But when day 60 draws near, York comes up short. He then goes to the owner and asks for an extension of time, just enough time to enter the upcoming turkey shoot he knows he can win.

York explains to the landowner that the man who shoots five perfect scores will win a whole beef critter. York explained that he intends to sell the beef critter to pay off the remainder of his debt. The landowner agreed to give him an extension of time. Meanwhile, he does win the contest but just as he does, the landowner arrives with Alvin's rival who himself has bought the land just to spite him. This was Alvin's Gethsemane. This was Alvin's test. Would he be able to forgive?

Alvin went to the two men who wronged him. First, to the man who sold him his land and next, to the man who bought the land just to spite him. Both men immediately believed York came seeking revenge. They were both fearful for what would happen next. But then Alvin York spoke the cleansing words to both men, "I'm a asking for your forgiveness."

That's it folks. Those are the words that can soften the heart of the oppressor. Those are the words that will change the heart of him who has been oppressed. But you have to go to the oppressor, face to face, one on one, and ask for his forgiveness.

In this example, Alvin York is clearly the one who was wronged. York did not do anything wrong. He went to the man who sold him his land and asked for an extension of time to finish paying the owner of the land the balance due. The owner agreed to give York that extension. But when the opportunity arose for another to purchase the land, immediately this rival bought the land just to spite him. York no doubt, initially had the same human emotions that anyone would have until that "spirit which passeth understanding (which is the Holy Ghost) stepped in and calmed York down. He then knew he should ask forgiveness of those who wronged him and that is what he did. When we ask forgiveness or forgive others, there is a quieting balm that comes to us to replace all the unkind feelings of revenge that seem to come after we have been wronged. "And the peace of God, which passseth all understanding, shall keep your hearts and minds through Christ Jesus" (Phillipians 4:7).

God requires us to ask forgiveness, not only of those we have wronged, but of those we have unkind feelings for because they have wronged us. The operative word is "forgiveness." We must ask it of those we have offended and we must offer it to those who have offended us. The screenplay for the motion picture, Sergeant York is so good and ahead of its time, as pertaining to teaching eternal truths that I thought it would be instructive to include that part of it that impressed me the most.

Let us examine that part of the script where York goes to the man who sold his land out from under him:

"Howdy, Mr. Tomkins.
- Look here. Stand where you are.
Don't you come any closer.
- Mr. Tomkins, I just want to...
- Come closer and I'll hit you.
No need of getting riled, Mr. Tomkins.
- I ain't a-looking for no trouble with you.
- What you doing around here?
- Well, I want to talk to you about...
- What about?
About Abraham.
That mule's legally mine.
You ain't got no claim on him.
Well, I ain't denying he's yours...
Stay where you are if you don't want to be laid out in two pieces.
Well, I was a-figuring on a-buying Abraham back.
-Buying him back?

- Yes, sir.
My mule's kind of poorly,
and something done happened to him
and I sure need a mule.
- Are you meaning it?
- Yes, sir.
No hard feelings?
- Shucks, no, Mr. Tomkins.
- Well, I'll be damned.
And... And there's one more thing.
I'm asking your forgiveness
for a-flaring up at you the way I done.
It were Satan a-speaking out of me.
Zeke was a-telling me, but I...
I couldn't believe him.
- About what?
- That you got religion.
- Well, that's a fact, Mr. Tomkins.
- Well, I'll be damned.
Well, I sure would like to be a-buying
that there mule back.
- You would, huh?
- Yeah.
- How much would you be asking for him?
- Well, let's see.
You said he was worth $40
and I allowed you $30.
That's right.
Well, you can have him back for $20.
Mr. Tomkins, Abraham's worth
a sight more than that.
Maybe he is,
but seeing as how I'm trying to do

the fair and square thing, Alvin, $20.
I reckon I know what you're thinking.
It's more blessed to give than to receive.
Maybe. Come on, get your mule.
And another thing, I'm gonna
give you back the clock you sold me.
-Yeah?
-Yeah, it don't run nohow."

York Then Confronts the Man Who Bought the Bottomland He Wanted to Own

"Howdy, Mr. Andrews.
- Howdy.
I'd kind of like to see Zeb,
are he hereabout?
Maybe he is.
I sure would like to have words with him.
You coming peaceful?
Yes, sir, Mr. Andrews.
I ain't looking for no trouble.
Zeb. Come out of there.
There he be.
Howdy.
What you'd be wanting with me,
Alvin York?
I want to talk to you, Zeb, about...
About that there piece of land.
I bought it, it's mine.
I know it, but...

Sure it's yours, Zeb, but...
But Nate Tomkins was...
Was a-figuring that...
I ain't caring
what Nate Tomkins was a-figuring.
- Well, Nate was just thinking...
- It's mine and I'm gonna keep it.
Well, sure it's yours, Zeb,
but if you'll only allow me to talk...
Ain't nobody a-holding you.
Oh, yes, they are.
Well, anyway, Nate was a-thinking
that your being so busy here,
maybe you need some extra help
on the other piece of land.
- Well, what's that got to do with you?
- Well, I'm asking you for the job.
- You mean you're aiming to work for me?
- I'd be if you allow me.
Well, shucks. That sure got me stumped.
I was a-buying that land just to spite you.
Well, I sure don't blame you none.
Well, maybe we can figure it
so you can sharecrop the piece.
Then you kind of be a-working for yourself.
No, I ain't asking for anything extra, Zeb.
Well, if you can farm that bottomland
like you've been doing the top,
I reckon that land will be yours
in a couple of seasons.
Well, with the help of the Lord,
I'll make you a good crop"

Finally, York Reports Back to Gracie, the Girl He Hopes to Marry

"Like I'm saying, Miss Gracie,
I ain't ever seen a prettier piece of land
than that there Andrews farm.
Corn is thicker than fur on a squirrel.
And I seen eight beef critters
a-grazing in the pasture there.
That are a lot of critters.
And that Zeb Andrews
sure are a forgiving man.
- Is he?
- Yes, sir.
Be sitting, Alvin.
- And a Christian man, if I ever seen one.
- Reckon so.
What I done to him that night
we were visiting you weren't right.
The devil was a-pushing me from behind.
It were too dark. I couldn't see.
I didn't have no call
to come twixt you and him.
What are you getting at, Alvin York?
All I'm aiming to say, Miss Gracie, is,
a upstanding man like Zeb Andrews
would make a girl a right smart husband.
- What's that?
- And.

And if you change your mind about Zeb,
well, I reckon I could...
- You could what?
- I could rightly understand.
Oh, you could, could you?
Lookee here, Alvin York,
if I wanted Zeb Andrews for a husband,
I reckon I could get him
without your acting so noble.
- I done kissed you, didn't I?
- Yes.
Well, I don't go around kissing men
I ain't gonna be a-marrying.
Now you be a-listening to me.
- Am I marrying a piece of land?
- Yes. No.
- Or a beef critter?
- No.
Or a field of corn?
No, it's you I'm marrying,
ain't nobody else in this here world.
- Are you hearing me?
- Yes.
Well, then don't you talk that way
to me again, Alvin!
- No.
- Don't you ever!
Oh!
The Lord sure do move
in mysterious ways" (The Screenplay for
Sergeant York is given the following credits:
Abem Finkel, Harry Chandlee, Howard Koch,
John Huston and Alvin C. York).

89

In the motion picture, and in real life, Alvin York gets the girl. In addition, the state of Tennessee builds a new home for him and gives him some of his own land. Will that happen for you if you forgive another for his trespasses against you? Perhaps, but that should not matter. What counts is that you have a promise from the Savior of the world, that if you first forgive another for his trespasses against you, your **Heavenly Father** will forgive you for your trespasses.

Asking forgiveness of one whom you have wronged is not the easiest thing to do for even the heartiest among us, but you can do it. Not many things that are good for us are easy to do. If life were easy, there wouldn't be any need to work at it because everything would be handed to us on a silver platter.

You may have to pray mightily for quite a while. You may have to fast more than just a little. You may find yourself buried in the scriptures from time to time to get yourself in the right frame of mind. But if you will ask God to soften your heart and give you the strength and desire to forgive offenders and ask forgiveness of others, it can be done.

In the simplest of terms, asking forgiveness of another and forgiving offenses, allows the atonement of Jesus Christ to work in your life. It doesn't matter if you were the offender or if you are completely innocent of any offense, the minute you even have feelings of disappointment let alone unkind feelings towards the offender, you become guilty of unkind feelings.

Asking forgiveness will soften your heart. Asking forgiveness is for you more than it is the offender because asking forgiveness will allow the Holy Ghost to make you a new creature in Christ. You can have God change your heart and give you a new heart, a heart that is teachable, broken and contrite. You will then have a heart free from anger, bitterness and unkind feelings.

Alvin York in Real Life

In the motion picture *Sergeant York,* Gary Cooper won the academy award for his heartwarming and very convincing portrayal of Alvin York. In real life, York was not struck by lightning. Alvin York changed his life from a hard drinking hell raiser because his friend, *Everett Delk* was killed in a bar fight causing York to re-assess his life. (From Wikipedia, the free encyclopedia).

Having the central character struck by lightning while riding his mule home in the pouring rain following a night of drinking without question, plays better on the silver screen. There are also the details of a bent rifle barrel and a steaming hot horseshoe from the heat of the lightening strike.

In point of fact, it matters little how the Almighty gets a man's attention enough to cause that man to change his life and come unto Christ.

It matters only that all men do come unto Christ and mend their ways or repent. But the movie has it right with the visual of the lightening striking Alvin York.

However, the incident within the motion picture that is the most powerful for me is not just when York forgives his neighbor for wronging him but his ability and willingness to ask forgiveness of his neighbor for the unkind feelings he held in his heart because his neighbor had wronged him. This is powerful stuff to come from a movie and it takes the motion picture *Sergeant York,* to a new level in filmmaking.

What Is the Responsibility of the Offended Individual?

He or she is required to forgive you with all of their heart and that's how it is supposed to work. But does it?

And if we are not doing this in God's way we need to correct ourselves from doing this the wrong way and invite the spirit of love and peace, which is the Holy Ghost, into everything we do. You will never be right with God until you apologize to all you have offended and until you forgive all those who have offended you.

How can you know that you are finally right with God? "If your heart condemns you, God is greater than your heart and knoweth all things. If your heart condemns you not; then you will have confidence in God" (1 John 3:20).

What if the Person Offended Does Not Forgive?

What if they decide they would rather hold a grudge and let that grudge simmer for years? What then? You many pray for them but they have their agency. They may choose to do whatever they wish. God will force no one "to do good" and God will force no man or woman to heaven.

You will remember as previously mentioned, those who will not forgive: will not be forgiven by God. From the Sermon on the Mount we read:

"For if ye forgive men their trespasses, your heavenly Father will also forgive you. But if ye forgive not men their trespasses, neither will your Father forgive your trespasses" (Matthew 6:14-15).

So, if you want to benefit from the blessings of the Lord, please forgo being stubborn, proud and unforgiving. Everything we do in this life, every decision we make, has its consequences, that's just the way it is.

Time for Some Self-Examination

Getting back now to that sage observation of James from long ago: "If any man offend not in word, the same is a perfect man" (James 3:2). More than one person has told me over the years that someone has offended them so much that they no longer wish to be a part of organized religion.

When I have asked them if they are ready to come back to God, although they may or may not have said it out loud to me, they have inferred this, "I will not come back until the person who offended me comes up to me and apologizes. The trouble is, if you wait for that to happen it may take a very long time. The other problem with that idea and attitude is, most of these folks still hold a grudge and continue to stay away from God even when the person who offended them does apologize.

This could be the time to ask yourself a question or two. Are you using another person's bad behavior and lack of sensitivity as an excuse and a reason to stop believing in God? Are you expecting the other fella to be perfect? No one is perfect, not even you. We just can't expect other people to be perfect anymore. We have to allow other folks to make mistakes. Life gets a lot easier to manage when we do. Therefore, everyone has flaws and imperfections. That is one of the reasons why we are here on earth. We are here to find our strengths and to find our weaknesses. The apostle Paul new something about weaknesses. Said he, referring to his weakness, "For this thing I besought the Lord thrice, that it might depart from me. And he said unto me, My grace is sufficient for thee for my strength is made perfect in weakness. Most gladly therefore will I rather glory in my infirmities; that the power of Christ may rest upon me. Therefore I take pleasure in infirmities, in reproaches, in necessities, in persecutions, in distresses for Christ's sake: for when I am weak, then am I strong" (2 Cor. 12:8-10).

If we come before God and admit to God that we have faults, God has promised to make our shortcomings become strong. Do you believe God? Paul said, "I can do all things through Christ which strengtheneth me" (Philippians 4:13). Do you trust God to keep his promise? Or are you still using what someone said or did to you long ago as an excuse to remove yourself from God instead of putting yourself back into the gospel of Jesus Christ so that you might be able to receive the blessings God is waiting to give you?

Holding a Grudge

Please stop holding a grudge. Please stop wanting to get even and seeking revenge. Have you finally figured out that everyone who lives on this earth is imperfect? Everyone has faults and weaknesses and imperfections and shortcomings. But here comes the shocker for some, remember, that also includes "little ole ME and little ole YOU." So if you are not perfect, if you have weaknesses and make mistakes, why do you insist and demand that others be perfect?

That is what you are doing you know, if you hold a grudge against those who have offended, dishonored, disrespected, or insulted you or hurt your feelings in any way. Have you ever considered how many people you have offended or insulted or dishonored, disrespected, or hurt their feelings, perhaps completely innocently, and without even knowing you have? Wake up boys and girls! Let the light of understanding, truth and love fill up your foggy brain, and soften your cold, cold heart. Stop it! Don't you realize that holding a grudge is hurting you more than it is hurting anyone else?

Stop singing, He or she "done me wrong," and try singing, "Please forgive that misguided soul who done me wrong and please help me to forgive them too. And even though I'd like to, pardon the phrase, 'drop kick them across America,' please help me to fast and pray and have a sense of humor and a spiritual understanding about all this so I can get on with my life."

This little poem may help:

"Oliver Wendell Cromwell Hyde one day, just up and died. But he did not find himself where he had hoped to reside when he reached the other side. When he opened his eyes he realized he was sitting next to the rich man from the parable of the Rich Man and Lazarus looking out across the vast expanse of an impassible gulf into the eyes of many who were poor in this life. Then Oliver Wendell Cromwell Hyde said, "Father Abraham what did I do that was wrong in my life to deserve such a fate now that I have died?"

Then Father Abraham replied,
"Do you not know, do you not yet realize?
You held onto a grudge all of your life, while you
were alive. You let it fester and simmer and burn
all the love from your heart so that no love within
you has survived. Instead of holding onto your
grudge you should have forgiven all who offended
you and trespassed against you while you were
alive. But because you chose to try and get even
you are here with all others who would not be
contrite. Yet the meek and the lowly and the poor
in spirit are with the poor man from the parable of
the Rich Man and Lazarus while you must suffer
until you can let your grudge subside."

There seems to be a great contradiction between the person who says, they know and love God; and yet still holds a festering grudge against another person who has done them wrong. If you want the Holy Ghost to be your constant companion; then forgive everyone and anyone who has done you wrong and ask God to forgive those who have wronged you. However, when anyone holds thoughts in his heart for just a minute about getting even with and doing harm to his neighbor, the Holy Ghost will flee from you about as fast as a robber will flee from you after he has taken everything you own that he wants.

How to Rid Yourself of Bad Feelings for Another

The only way for you to get rid of your

grudge and get that bitterness and venom in your heart from being offended, out of your heart is this: You will just have to get down on your knees and ask God the Eternal Father to give you the strength to humble yourself enough to truly come unto Christ and take his yoke upon you and let the atonement of Jesus Christ change your heart and give you a new heart.

There is no other way. You cannot be your own Savior. You cannot receive the blessings of God by staying home stewing and sulking and thinking you are getting even by staying away from God. God is everywhere. God made everywhere and God made you. And because God made you, God loves you more than you may ever know or understand in this life. God wants you to come back into the gospel of Jesus Christ. Won't you let the Savior of the World back into your life? It is impossible not to get better with Christ in your life.

Tolerate Correction

When you are corrected in public, do you hear yourself thanking the person who has corrected you? This afternoon I was sitting next to someone in authority who was corrected in public. When he was corrected he said, "Thank you for correcting me to the person who had corrected him. One observing this behavior could not help but get the idea that the person who was corrected was living on a much higher level than most. Those in observance of this man's behavior could not help but to get the immediate impression that the man who was corrected was doing far more than tolerating it. He gave the impression to all that he invited those around him to correct him should it be necessary and that he appreciated it.

God tells us that we should be willing to bear correction. And we should. Here is what will make that easier to do: "For whom the Lord loveth he correcteth; even as a father the son in whom he delighteth" (Proverbs 3:12).

So if you are being corrected a lot, God must love you a lot. Having a sense of humor will also help all of us to tolerate correction. Mark Twain once said, "Humor is the great thing, the saving thing after all. The minute it crops up, all our hardnesses yield, all of our irritations and resentments flit away, and a sunny spirit takes their place."

By the way, if you are just going through the motions of life by waking, eating, sleeping and waking up again, there is a pretty good chance that no one will ever notice you, so you will probably never be corrected for anything.

But if you spend your life trying to do good, trying to help others, live with and love all of God's children, now you pose a threat to the Adversary, and he will do his part to provide opposition in your life.

Correcting Others

If you feel you absolutely must correct someone in public, do it this way. Walk up to the person and whisper in their ear so that others will not overhear what you will be saying. Please remember to correct others with love and respect for them in your heart. Never correct someone in public in anger. Should you do this, it will be you who will need help and not them. If you are in the habit of so doing, you probably need some anger management classes. Yes, you probably need some professional help. Anger, resentment, judgment and treating others without respect does not come from God. Such behavior comes from below and not from above.

When all is said and done there will be precious few times in our lives when we need to correct another one of God's children and most particularly, in public. One example would be if a child were playing with a loaded gun. Another would be if a military leader were about to give the final launch sequences to a nuclear missile aimed at one of the major cities of the world. Unless someone is about to do something to endanger another person's life, it is almost always best to hold your peace. The next time you find yourself wishing to give someone a piece of your mind, stop. Consider if you will, that the words you are about to speak can never be called back. Now consider if you lash out at someone in anger, you will not only be damaging the other person but you will also cause harm to yourself.

To illustrate, we have not yet learned the language of all animals. Not everyone under-stands that a dog that barks all night may be in pain. That was the case with one particular dog. The neighbor who was kept awake all night was just itching to give her neighbor a piece of her mind when morning came but she did not. She later found out that this dog was dying of cancer. Her neighbors could not afford to pay for a veterinarian. She said she was glad she did not complain to her neighbor. The neighbor who did not complain later had her own dog die of cancer.

There will be times when we will have no control over what happens around us. Will we complain to those who annoy us? Will we insist upon giving them a piece of our mind? Or will we try and be understanding and realize there could be a perfectly good reason why all of God's children behave the way they do? When it comes to interacting with all of God's creations, may we realize that, "Every living thing has feelings and should be loved" (from Prince Galem and the Golden Key, Copyright © 2016 by Ron Bartalini).

God's Way to Continue After Correcting People

There is still something that almost everyone leaves out of this correction business. God's way of correcting people is not man's way. Man's way is to just correct someone and be done with it. God teaches us to show and tell he who was corrected-that you love and appreciate them after they have been corrected. Where is the showing forth of love? If it is not there, you will be esteemed to be that man's enemy.

Behaving this way is not a part of the gospel of Jesus Christ! When you correct someone please, do not be the one who forgets to show forth an increase in love after they have been corrected. This manifestation of your love for the corrected person should not end. Showing an increase in love for them should continue. Everything we do in this life should be done with love.

This shows the person who was corrected that you are a man of God; otherwise the person who was corrected will consider you an enemy. If you do not correct people in God's way, you probably have no business correcting anyone until you first correct yourself.

James has reminded us: "But the wisdom that is from above is first pure, then peaceable gentle, and easy to be entreated, full of mercy and good fruits, without partiality, and without hypocrisy. And the fruit of righteousness in sown in peace of them that make peace" (James 3:17-18).

What To Do When You Are Falsely Accused

Now let us consider another scenario. This time someone you don't even know, someone you have never met says something to your boss or to your military commander or to a leader or someone in charge about you that isn't true. The person in question did not come to you and tell you. The person who has accused you doesn't know you. The person has never met you. He doesn't take time to meet you but he goes directly to a leader or to the boss or military commander or the person in charge, and the person in charge then calls you in and tells you all about it. Now what do you do? Do you get angry? Do you begin to hate this person? Do you seek revenge? Do you harbor ill feelings? Do you hold a grudge for this person? It should be pretty difficult to have any of those feelings for someone you have never met and don't even know.

The person who has been accused may wish to meet their accuser and say to them: "Please excuse me for anything I may have said or done to offend you. I ask your forgiveness. I welcome correction, God has said: "For he whom the Lord loveth, he correcteth even as a father the son in who he delighteth" (Proverbs 3:12). But I am afraid you have me at a disadvantage. I don't know you, and you do not know me, and yet you have accused me of doing something I know I did not do, to a boss, or a commander or a leader.

He who has been accused may wish to ask the accuser: Did you see me do the thing? Was it someone else who saw the thing done and then told you about it? If that was the case, that would be hearsay and hearsay is not admissible in a court of law. If you reported the thing, someone else saw to a leader, that would be hearsay three times removed by the time it got back to me. How long ago was it that you or someone else saw this thing? Why am I hearing about it from a leader and not from you? Why did I not here about it back when you or someone else saw the thing? When does he who is accused get to defend himself? What happened to, "innocent until proven guilty?"

Nowhere does it say in scripture: "Men shall be tattle tales. Men shall call the man's boss or leader or military commander and tell that person about the man's misgivings."

Allow People to Make Mistakes

If people did not make mistakes there would be no erasers. There would be no ejection seats for fighter pilots, seat belts or air bags for drivers of automobiles. Ships also, would carry no lifeboats or life rafts. If writers were able to write their works perfectly the first time they began to write, there would be no need for re-writes or editors.

Judge Not

You cannot judge another man until you have walked a mile in his shoes (moccasins) and then you won't want to. The truth is, only God knows what is in another man's heart. Everyone has a reason for what they do. People tend to do what they do because of the traditions of their fathers and because of their own life experiences. We must remember that all men and women get to choose for themselves. The path to follow is to accept all of God's children as they are and where they are in their own eternal progression now.

Let us follow the admonition of our beloved Savior when he said, "Judge not, that ye be not judged. For with what judgment ye judge, ye shall be judged: and with what measure ye mete, it shall be measured to you again. And why beholdest thou the mote that is in thy brother's eye, but considerest not the beam that is in thine own eye? Or how wilt thou say to thy brother, Let me pull out the mote out of thine eye: and, behold, a beam is in thine own eye? Thou hypocrite, first cast out the beam out of thine own eye; and then shalt thou see clearly to cast out the mote out of thy brother's eye" (Matthew 7:1-5).

The Devastating Effects of Gossip and Rumors

Few things in life have the capability to destroy another person's character and reputation faster than gossip and rumors. The problem with gossip and rumors is, people tend to believe what they hear about others even though that which they hear is a bold-faced lie. Meanwhile, the damage has been done and it is difficult for the person so damaged to regain their credibility. Consider the person who has been falsely imprisoned for a crime they did not commit. Only God could sort this out and administer justice to the victim of such an injustice and meet out proper punishment to those who were the innocent man's accusers.

The lesson here is, stay out of the judgment business. It is not your business. It is God's business. If you do not have something good to say about someone, do not speak. The next time you find yourself talking about someone, check yourself. Hold your peace. Remember, people tend to believe what they hear about others.

Hearsay

Hearsay is "unofficial information gained or acquired from another and not part of one's direct knowledge" (From Webster's Dictionary). Hearsay is inadmissible in a court of law and we should pay no attention to it. Hearsay begins with rumor and it ends with judging another because of unsubstantiated rumors. If you were not there as an eye witness or if you did not hear with your own ears, you do not know what happened. When five or more people have heard a story about someone or something by the time the story reaches you that would be hearsay five or more times removed. Virtually everyone on occasion embellishes the truth until what they indicate is so far from reality there is no truth remaining. To illustrate, when I was serving at the Religious Retreat Center in Cam Rahn Bay, Vietnam, I was privileged to teach what was the equivalent of Sunday school classes to visiting servicemen from the Air Force, Army and Navy. I developed one particular class that demonstrated how something spoken about someone can begin innocently enough, but after it is heard and repeated by a dozen or more people, that which was first spoken can evolve into something quite different.

Hearsay Illustrated

I began by having each class of 12 or more servicemen sit down and form a circle. I then invited the man to my left to stand up and introduce himself to the class by only stating his name. I asked the class to try and remember his name because they would only hear it once. The class was told not to write it down or to talk to one another. Then I explained they would not hear the rest of the instructions until the man to their right whispered them in their ear. I then whispered instructions to the man who had just introduced himself to the class. He was told to whisper in the ear of the man to his left, "what his talents were, what he likes to do now, where his hometown is located, what his education is and what he would like to do when he returned home. He was told to give those exact instructions to the man to his left and so on. When the last man in the circle heard his instructions, he was invited to stand and tell the class all about the first man. I wish that you, the reader, could have been there to hear how the identity of the man who introduced himself changed by the time the last man gave his report. This is a great exercise to demonstrate how gossip can turn into rumors and how rumors can become hearsay. Gossip, rumors and hearsay can have a devastating effect on the lives of others because the truth can change after it is passed along to many people. Furthermore, far too many believe that which they hear from another to be the truth. But that which they have heard from another is usually nothing more than hearsay.

Forgiving Yourself

Jesus has already offered himself a ransom for your sins. Jesus has already paid the price for your sins by suffering in Gethsemane, and then by laying down his life on the cross at Calvary and by and through the infinite atonement of Jesus Christ. Will you put the atonement of Jesus Christ to shame? Satan walks up and down this earth like a roaring lion waiting to sift you as wheat, but Christ has prayed not only for the apostle Peter, Jesus has also prayed for you that your faith would fail not. Will you not pray for yourself? We have this unshakable and timeless promise from the Almighty: "For God so loved the world, that he gave his only begotten Son, that whosoever believeth in him should not perish, but have everlasting life" (John 3:17). Will you believe in Christ? Will you believe that he is, that he has conquered death that he lives today and that he came to the earth to save you, the sinner? But we are all sinners.

Will you then believe in yourself? Will you forgive yourself, even as Christ will forgive you if you will believe on him and acknowledge before God that you are a sinner?

Having Regrets Because of Past Mistakes

One of my friends just sent me this explanation of his regrets from making past mistakes, "I came to realize recently that I had a bitter cup experience from missing Med School, missing a chance to start a business, loosing two wonderful ladies. All of these *great losses* due to stupidity and errors on my part have led to a bitter cup for me, which endures to this day. I think about each of these great losses several times a day. This is my bitter cup. I hate this more than anything, but it has fashioned me over and over. I brushed off a strong prompting about Med School, and it was terribly wrong. These things happened through my own stupidity, but it is part of life. I thank God every day for the wonderful blessings I have received in spite of these things."

The "Bitter Cup" experience is part of our eternal progression in this life.

Learn from Past Mistakes

It is important that we learn from our past mistakes but not dwell on them. Is there anyone out there who has not made a mistake? We are all imperfect. We are all here on earth to learn from our mistakes, not to be intimidated by them. If Edison did not learn from his mistakes and move on and continue to try and discover the right and correct filament that would make his light bulb work, the world may still be in darkness. Stop dwelling on past mistakes and get out there and start anew. Let the past go, leave it alone, say goodbye to it. You cannot go back in time and you are not supposed to. Move forward. Move ahead. Be happy and grateful for a new day. Believe in God. Believe in yourself and ask God to help you to make your dreams come true. Then undertake activities to do all you can personally. Don't expect God to do for you what you can do yourself.

Can I Conquer My Weakness By Myself?

Will you be able to conquer your greatest weaknesses by yourself? Probably not, but even if you were able to do that it will take much longer than if you had God's help. However, if you invite the Savior of the world into your life and humble yourself and ask for God's help, I promise you he will help you conquer your weaknesses and make weak things become strong unto you and he will do that for you much sooner than you may think. The key is to truly humble yourself, confess your weaknesses to God and then ask the God of heaven and earth to help you conquer yourself.

Remember, faith is not just saying that you believe. You must show God you believe by those things which you do. You must live as if you already see and hear those things manifested before you, which you hope are true.

I promise you that if you will show forth an ounce of faith, God will make up the difference. Jesus gave a secret of the ages when he declared, "For verily I say unto you, If ye have faith as a grain of mustard seed, ye shall say unto this mountain, Remove hence to yonder place; and it shall remove; and nothing shall be impossible unto you. " (Matthew 17:20). Just how big is a grain of mustard seed? The average mustard seed will range from one to two millimeters. Therefore, many mustard seeds will easily fit in the palm of your hand. To illustrate, 1.2 millimeters is equal to one twentieth of an inch. (From Wikipedia, the free encyclopedia).

God's Children Can Have Multiple Talents

Have you ever considered that you may have more than one talent and more than one set of skills? Don't underestimate yourself. Don't sell yourself short. Ask yourself, what is it I can do to make this a better world in which to live? Then ask God and he will direct your path. Focus on the poor and the helpless not on the rich and famous and those who don't need help. But even the rich and famous can use a sympathetic ear from time to time. You may also wish to answer these questions: What have I done to help my neighbors recently? What have I done today?

Timing

It is an easy thing to forget that God's timing is not necessarily man's timing. Most men and women want what they want now; they are not willing to plan for it, to prepare for it, to wait for it. Someone said to me long ago, "When the time is right." I have learned since, that we can make the time right by drawing closer to God. Pride enables people to persist in believing they can do anything they wish to do on their own. They continue to keep God out of their lives. The Son of God is standing at the proverbial front door of your heart. Will you open the door to your heart and let him in? James has written, "Draw nigh to God and he will draw nigh to you" (James 4:8). Do you understand? Will you believe that it is you who must take the first step? And when you have let God in your life, you must continue to let the Lord be a part of your every decision, not just once in awhile. Study things out. Do your research. Put in the time it takes to do your due diligence and then watch things change as you include God in your decisions after you are prepared to do so.

Learn to ask intelligent questions of the Almighty. God has the answer to all of your questions but he will not give them to you on a silver platter. For those who take life for granted they seem to end up with the same fate as the "rich man" in the parable of the rich man and Lazarus.

What have you done to draw nearer to God this year that you have never done before? Are you studying the word of God in his holy scriptures? Are you helping your neighbors? Are you paying an honest tithe? Are you praying more often? Do you visit the fatherless and widows? Do you help the poor in whatever ways you can? Have you ever comforted a stranger or visited someone in prison? Do you visit precious children who are terminally ill?

How can you expect God to bless you if you continue to do the same things?

But when you begin to help the poor and focus on doing that which has been mentioned above, God will help you to forgive those who have trespassed against you. God will change your heart that you might be able to ask forgiveness of those you have offended. Best of all, and not surprisingly, God will help you to forgive yourself.

Facing Life's Trials

Everyone Will Be Given Trials, But None We Cannot Handle

My neighbor just said when I asked him how life was going for him, "This isn't right," referring to doctors not being able to find a cure for his wife's ailments. I was reminded of two things. First, we sign off and agree to face the problems we have in this life before we come to the earth. And second, we are not given problems we cannot deal with. Someone else may not be able to do it but we will never be given trials we cannot handle.

I recently saw a young crippled girl in one of my favorite restaurants one afternoon. She was making her way across the floor on her crutches. Her body was twisted but she was navigating the floor with a smile on her face. I thought if I could just do what the apostle Peter did for one crippled man, I would do it. Peter once said, "Silver and gold, have I none; but such as I have give I thee: In the name of Jesus Christ of Nazareth rise up and walk" (Acts 3:7). Then Peter "took him by the right hand, and lifted him up: and immediately his feet and ankle bones received strength. And he leaping up stood, and walked, and entered with them into the temple, walking, and leaping, and praising God" (Acts 3:7-8).

But just as I had that thought, the Holy Ghost spoke to me, as clearly as one man speaks to another and yet it was not in an audible voice. It was without words, heard not with ears but by that still small voice you can hear clearly in your mind and in your heart. That marvelous spirit, said to me, "Hold back, do nothing, she is well enough. She is happy and she is content with her lot in life. She agreed to live her life with her handicap before she came to this earth and all is well with her and she will be eternally blessed." It is because of that experience that I know, God will never give us a problem or handicap or trial we cannot deal with and that many of us if not all, have agreed to face our trials, before we came to this earth by raising our right arm to the square and agreeing to face our own particular challenges in this life.

How to Forgive Yourself

The most difficult thing to do for some is to forgive oneself. I heard a story long ago about two brothers who were out "off road driving" having fun. There was an unforeseen accident and one of the brothers lost his life. The brother who survived the accident was unable to forgive himself for causing the death of his brother. But in reality, that which has just been described was an accident. I have heard other stories of more than one soldier who was in a firefight and could not protect one his comrades who died in the battle and that soldier blames himself and is unable to forgive himself. The man who holds himself responsible may be thinking about what the Savior taught us regarding the greatest kind of love when Jesus declared, "Greater love hath no man than this, that a man lay down his life for a friend" (John 15:13). The soldier in question should realize that God knows the intent of your heart and that is enough. Forgive yourself because God has already forgiven you. To the adulteress Jesus proclaimed, "Neither do I condemn thee, Go and sin no more" (John 8:11).

The Unpardonable Sin

Did you know that all manner of sin shall be forgiven except the unpardonable sin which is, blasphemy against the Holy Ghost. From the gospel according to Matthew we read, "Wherefore I say unto you, All manner of sin and blasphemy shall be forgiven unto men: but the blasphemy against the Holy Ghost shall not be forgiven unto men. And whosoever speaketh a word against the Son of man, It shall be forgiven him: but whosoever speaketh against the Holy Ghost, it shall not be forgiven him, neither in this world, neither in the world to come" (Matthew 12:31-32).

The first thing one who cannot forgive

himself should understand is that Jesus Christ has paid the price for your sins. The Savior of the world has done this by and through the infinite atonement. James taught, "faith without works is dead" (James 2:20. In other words, we may have faith in Christ but if we do not act on our belief, our faith in Christ will do us no good. The question now arises," What must one do to claim the marvelous gifts of the atonement and the grace of Jesus Christ?"

Jesus gave us the answer when he said, "If ye love me keep my commandments. And I will pray the Father, and he shall give you another Comforter, that he may abide with you for ever; Even the Spirit of truth; whom the world cannot receive, because it seeth him not, neither knoweth him: but ye know him; for he dwelleth with you and shall be in you" (John 14:17).

"He that hath my commandments, and keepeth them, he it is that loveth me: and he that loveth me shall be loved of my Father, and I will love him, and will manifest myself to him" (John 14:21).

"But the Comforter, which is the Holy Ghost, whom the Father will send in my name, he shall teach you all things, and bring all things to your remembrance, whatsoever I have said unto you" (John 14:26). God has given mankind the Holy Ghost knowing that he would not always be with us. The Holy Ghost can be our friend, our teacher, our Comforter and our constant companion.

The Holy Ghost should be at the top of everyone's bucket list to become a permanent part, of the lives of all of God's children.

What Commandments Should We Keep to Enter Heaven?

A certain man of import, a Pharisee named Nicodemus and ruler of the Jews was given that answer by the Savior almost two thousand years ago. Jesus answered him by saying, "Except a man be born of water and of the spirit, he cannot enter the kingdom of God" (John 3:5). The apostle Paul asked a group of believers, "Have ye received the Holy Ghost since you believed?" (Acts 19:2). They answered him, "We have not so much as heard of the Holy Ghost." (Acts 19:2).

Some folks expect God to bless them when they do nothing more than ask. Although that is a good start, a wonderful start, it takes a little more that just asking. Change begins and ends with you. Climb up to higher ground. Do something you have never done before to show God you honor him and love him. Make the change and God will bless you for it.

The most reliable data available concerning the number of Christian churches in the world today comes from David B. Barrett. It is entitled, World Christian Encyclopedia, and published by Oxford University Press.

The 2001 edition, successor to his 1982 first edition, which took a decade to compile, identifies 10,000 distinct religions, of which 150 have 1 million or more followers. **Within Christianity, he counts 33,820 denominations**. Imagine, there are almost 34,000 versions of the gospel of Jesus Christ!

Barrett also calculates religious populations for the *Encyclopedia Britannica* Book of the Year, standard estimates that are used in turn by the *World Almanac* and innumerable journalists. Such numbers are always debatable, but they're the best available. "We don't really have any rivals," Barrett says. "That's the problem."

Title: *World Christian Encyclopedia : a comparative survey of churches and religions in the modern world*
Authors: David B. Barrett, George T. Kurian, Todd M. Johnson.
Edition: 2nd ed.
Published: Oxford ; New York : Oxford University Press, 2001.
Description: 2 v. : ill., col. maps ; 32 cm.
Notes: Includes bibliographical references and indexes.
Contents: v. 1. The world by countries : religionists, churches, ministries.
v. 2. The world by segments : religions, peoples, languages, cities, topics. (from Richard N. Ostling, Associated Press, 19 May 2001).

With respect and admiration for all of you, Jesus requires very little of those who believe on him to enter the kingdom of heaven. But basic to accomplishing this end is the need to be baptized in the name of Jesus Christ and to receive the Holy Ghost in the name of Jesus Christ.

Understanding the Process

What does the need for you to be baptized and receive the gift of the Holy Ghost have to do with the Father forgiving you of your sins when you have forgiven others of their sins against you? Answer. It is all part of the process.

You have seen this process unfold in the lives of John Newton, Jean Val Jean and Saul of Tarsus who became the apostle Paul. We have continued to explore the lives of modern day men of renown including Captain Louis Zamperini and Sergeant Alvin York. The process continues to consist of the same steps perhaps not in the same order because all of God's children are different yet the process remains the same. One conclusion persists, learning how to forgive another, to ask forgiveness of another and to ultimately forgive oneself is a process that will take time according to the effort each man or woman puts forth.

Granted, only Saul of Tarsus from the preceding accounts was baptized but the fact remains that Jesus set down the need for baptism and receiving the gift of the Holy Ghost in the records left to us within the scriptures.

The men we have explored did what they could with the light and truth they had at the time they lived. But you now have more light and truth to help you finish the process of learning how to forgive, to ask forgiveness and to forgive yourself. What will you do with that light and truth? Will you do what the Savior of the world has asked us to do? Will you repent and be baptized and receive the gift of the Holy Ghost?

The apostle Paul understood the importance of following the complete process so well that he emphasized the truth of the necessity of baptism for all men and women even for the dead with these words:

"Else what shall they do who are baptized for the dead, if the dead rise not at all? why are they then baptized for the dead" (1 Corinthians 15:29)?

Yes, Paul knew that all must be baptized to enter the kingdom of heaven. He himself was indeed baptized as we have read earlier discussing his life. Would the Son of the living God give a commandment that he would not also provide a means of keeping? He certainly would not. There were people being baptized by John the Baptist and others when Jesus walked the earth. There was a temple in Jerusalem during the Savior's mortal ministry. The scripture above is referring to living people being baptized for the dead during this time.

Jesus said to the thief on the cross, "today thou shalt be with me in paradise" (Luke 23:43).

Within the parable of the "Rich Man and Lazarus" we read about Lazarus entering paradise. If these men were not baptized while they lived on the earth they would need to have someone living on earth be baptized for them by proxy. The commandment of the necessity of baptism to enter the kingdom of heaven has been given and it has not changed.

Living people are being baptized all over the world today with God's authority. Living people are being baptized in behalf of the dead in holy temples all over the world today. Why is this so? Answer, because it is part of the process to get to heaven. Remember, Jesus said: "except a man be born of water and of the Spirit, he cannot enter the kingdom of God" (John 3:5).

How Should I Be Baptized?

Will sprinkling do? When Jesus was baptized by John the Baptist the scripture records, "And Jesus, when he was baptized went straightway out of the water:" The Lord could not have come up out of the water unless he was first, under the water. Therefore, to be baptized correctly, one must go down under the water, signifying death and then come up out of the water, signifying a re-birth and one's sins being washed away.

The Authority of God to Baptize Is Required

"No man taketh this honor unto himself, but he who has been called of God, as was Aaron" (Hebrews 5:4).

There was one who wanted to buy the authority of God. Peter said unto him, "thy money perish with thee, for thou hast thought to buy the authority of God with money" (Acts 8:20).

To be baptized correctly; one must be baptized by another who has the authority of God. The questions should be asked, "Where did you get your authority to baptize? From whence cometh your priesthood? When Jesus called his twelve apostles, he called them forth and laid his hands on their heads and ordained them. When that was done, those twelve special witnesses of Jesus Christ had the authority of God to act in his name. No one who has not been baptized in the name of Jesus Christ and received the Holy Ghost, in the name of Jesus Christ can be called by his holy name at the last day. The preceding is basic to showing God we love him by keeping his commandments.

In addition to this we have the words of Christ, which inspired this book as basic to keeping God's commandments. You may wish to think of obeying the following words of our Lord and Savior as an insurance policy. Forgiving another will most certainly "insure" you will be forgiven by the Father. *"And forgive us our debts, as we forgive our debtors. For if we forgive men their trespasses, your heavenly Father will also forgive you: But if ye forgive not men their trespasses, neither will your Father forgive your trespasses" (Matthew 6:12; 14-15).*

Now that we know which of God's commandments to keep, let us have the courage and conviction to keep them. When we do, God will bless us to be able to forgive ourselves. How do I claim the benefits of the atonement of our Savior? You have no doubt, heard the saying, "don't tell me, show me." It is that way with the gospel of Jesus Christ. Jesus has said, "If ye love me, keep my commandments" as we have just read. In other words, if you love the Savior of the world, show him by keeping his commandments.

Put God to the Test

How can you possibly know if what has been outlined herein is the truth? How can you know if what you are reading is indeed what the Savior of the world would have you do? How can you know once and for all that there is a God in heaven and that he loves you? Have you ever bothered to ask? Have you ever bothered to get down on your knees and offer a simple and sincere prayer to God?

God will probably never come down from heaven and stand beside you and tell you he is God but your Heavenly Father will reveal himself to you in a way that you and you alone will know that he is real and that he does exist.

People generally behave the way they do because of the traditions of their fathers. Folks usually believe what they believe because that is what their parents believe or that is what the majority of the community believes. However, every man should find out the truth of all things for himself from God. Jesus has told us how to do that.

The Master has told us, "If ye love me, keep my commandments. And I will pray the Father, and he shall give you another Comforter, that he may abide with you forever. Even the Spirit of truth; whom the world cannot receive, because it seeth him not, neither knoweth him: but ye know him: for he dwelleth with you, and shall be in you.

Put God to the test. Ask God to reveal the truth to you and he will. If you will ask God, he will answer you. But you have to ask sincerely and with real intent. You have to really want to know. You cannot pray a casual prayer and expect God to answer you. Further, how many times will you pray to get your answers? Will you pray once or will you continue to pray, and search the word of God and even fast and pray until you not only get an answer but you have a personal experience with the Holy Ghost? Remember, God answers prayers today by and through living people, angels from heaven and by the gift and power of the Holy Ghost.

The prophet Joel has told us: "Your old men shall dream dreams, your young men shall see visions" (Joel 2:28). How will God answer you? You may hear that still, small, perfectly audible voice of the Holy Ghost in your mind and in your heart while you are awake.

When you have a personal experience with the Holy Ghost you will know forever that God lives and that he loves you and you will never be able to deny that again. Remember, the adversary, who is the devil and our common enemy is not able to imitate the Holy Ghost. Although he can appear as an angel of light, and can deceive us in countless ways, he cannot fill your soul with peace and hope and love or imitate the feeling of God's love that the Holy Ghost will cause you to feel as he descends upon you. Only the Holy Ghost can make you feel those feelings.

How can you know for yourself if you should be baptized? Ask God and he will answer you but remember Jesus was baptized by John the Baptist to set the example for all of mankind. Yes, you must be baptized to enter the kingdom of God. That was the instruction the Savior gave to Nicodemus.

How can you know for yourself which of all the churches you should join? You only need to ask God with a sincere prayer with real intent to know and God will answer you. But remember, the true church of Jesus Christ must bear his holy name. Otherwise, it could not be his church. Please also remember, Jesus was buried under the water when he was baptized, by John the Baptist and then he was raised up out of the water. Please also remember that without God's authority to baptize, God will not recognize your baptism as being valid.

When you pray, remember to ask specific and intelligent questions then God will answer you in a way that you will be able to understand. Praying and asking God about these things is not rocket science, anyone can do it. But you must take the time to ask God sincerely if you expect to get an answer. I like this timeless wisdom given to us by James. It is the ageless recipe for obtaining an answer from God:

"If any of you lack wisdom, let him ask of God, that giveth to all men liberally and upbraideth not, and it shall be given him.
But let him ask in faith, nothing wavering.

For he that wavereth is like a wave of the sea, driven with the wind and tossed.

For let not that man think that he shall receive anything of the Lord" (James 1:5-7).

Will God Forgive You?

Yes. "For God sent not his Son into the world to condemn the world; but that the world through him might be saved" (John 3:17). "For God so loved the world, that he gave his only begotten Son, that whosoever believeth in him should not perish but have everlasting life" (John 3:16).

Will God Forget Your Sins?

Yes. "And their sins and iniquities I will remember no more" (Hebrews 10:17). See also,

Isaiah 43:25; Hebrews 8:12).

Forgiving Yourself

Concerning the past mistakes you have made, let them go. Today is a brand new day. Let the past be over and done with. Forgive yourself because if you keep God's commandments as just outlined, you may be certain God will forgive you.

Learn to Love Yourself

It will be difficult to forgive yourself if you do not first, love yourself. The reason most people are unable to love themselves is because they are hiding some deep, dark secret from a past transgression. They do not love themselves because they are secretly still ashamed of a past mistake. The truth is, no one will be able to fully and completely love themselves and thereby forgive themselves without first making their life right with God. How long will you choose to wait to do that?

The way to do this is straight forward enough. You must first acknowledge that you too are a sinner. Then you must confess your sins and forsake them. The scriptures explain, "He that covereth his sins shall not prosper: but whoso confesseth and forsaketh them shall have mercy" (Proverbs 28:13). That is great advise but for so many, they find themselves confessing and forsaking the same sins again and again. Here is a simple idea that may change all that.

Take one of your shortcomings at a time but decide that this time you will conquer that weakness once and for all so that you never have to look back and start all over again trying to win the victory over it. For example, if you are having trouble paying tithing, instead of fighting with trying to live that commandment decide that you will not just pay your tithing but that each month you will pay a little extra than that which is required. You may then apply this same idea of doing a little more than God asks of us to conquering each one of your weaknesses.

When you have dealt with your sins and properly repented, your conscience will be clear, you will then begin to feel good about yourself. You can then learn to focus on the good that is in you. Now you can begin to love yourself and with God's help you will be able to forgive yourself.

A good goal to set for yourself would be for you to be able to read these verses from the book of Psalms and say to yourself, that scripture applies to me:

"Who shall ascend into the hill of the LORD? or who shall stand in his holy place? He that hath clean hands, and a pure heart; who hath not lifted up his soul unto vanity, nor sworn deceitfully. He shall receive the blessing from the LORD, and righteousness from the God of his salvation" (Psalms 24:4)

The Need to Forgive Re-Visited

Whether we like it or not, we are not in the judgment business. We are not in the getting even business or the revenge business either. We are all in the "forgiveness" business. If we fail to understand this and act upon it, we will be missing one of the great lessons of life and as a result of our misgiving, we will be sadly lacking in wisdom and understanding while we are alive.

Forgiving Another Is Not Easy

To forgive another for trespassing against you may be one of the most difficult things you will ever do and yet it must be done if you hope for God to forgive you of your sins. You deserve to be treated with respect. You deserve to be treated fairly and not lied to. You deserve not to be cheated or betrayed. Yet there are people out there who will take advantage of you any way they can. Every man and woman has "their own" agenda. Unfortunately, the agenda of many is to look out for number one and seize every opportunity to take advantage of their neighbors.

Our task in life is forgive them all for every infraction and offense.

Having a Broken Heart and a Contrite Spirit

The final objective of this exercise regarding, "The Power of Forgiveness," is this, we must surrender our will to the Father's will. When Jesus faced his final moment of decision to do the Father's will and offer himself a ransom for the sins of all mankind, the Savior made one final petition to his Father saying, "Father, if it be thy will, remove this cup from me, nevertheless, not my will but thine be done" (Luke 22:42). When a man or a woman is able to pray that prayer sincerely, that person will begin to understand the sacrifice our beloved Savior would have us make to him and that is, "a broken heart and a contrite spirit."

He who has a broken heart and a contrite spirit is humble. You then become like a little child; you are teachable. You are meek and lowly. The meek will inherit the earth (See Matthew 5:5). The proud however, are numbered among the wicked and they shall be as stubble. The proud shall be burned at the Lord's triumphant return to the earth. "For, behold, the day cometh, that shall burn as an oven; and all the proud, yea, and all that do wickedly, shall be stubble: and the day that cometh shall burn them up, saith the Lord of hosts, that it shall leaven them neither root nor branch" (Malachi 4:1).

But if we can manage to surrender our will to the Father's will, the way Jesus did, then everything changes. We can become a new creature in Christ. He can change our heart and give us a new heart and in time, we can actually no longer have the desire to sin, but have only the desire to do good continually. This is possible. Then we can begin to understand what Jesus meant when he said, "the sacrifices of God are a broken spirit, a broken and contrite heart" (Psalms 51:17). And when we are teachable, we will become as little children, and our lives will take on a whole new meaning.

Did you know that God can literally change your heart and give you a new heart? God can give you a heart that only desires to do good continually. God can do this for you if you allow him to. But you must take the first step.

God has given you your "will" or the ability to choose for yourself. When the day dawns that you are able to say to God, "Father in heaven, I know thou hast given me my will to do whatsoever I choose to do, but I freely give my will back to thee. I know that thou knowest all things and surely thou dost know what is best for me. I will not stop making my own decisions in life but I now desire to do only what thou would have me do." Then God will be able to change your heart and give you a new heart, one that will eventually only desire to do good.

Having a mighty change of heart does not happen in a day. Unless you are Saul of Tarsus and you suddenly see a light and hear a voice from heaven, changing your heart from what it now is, will take some time. Allowing Christ to change your heart and give you a new heart requires effort, on your part. It is a process.

Many seem to believe that God will change your heart with no effort or commitment from you other than asking God to do so for you. I just don't believe this is the way it works at all. This requires many small acts of kindness. An anthill is built one grain of sand at a time. Over a long enough period of time, an anthill can grow to a considerable height. Refining a man's soul and shaping his heart can take a lifetime of small acts of kindness until such behavior becomes second nature.

The desire to only wish to do good continually comes from God. That will always be a good thing for all men to experience. Changing one's heart also changes one's disposition. It softens the rough edges of a man's character. When that happens to you, you will be less likely to get angry and more inclined to be kind. You will have more mercy and understanding and thereby be better equipped to forgive others and to ask forgiveness of others.

More than one person has asked me how long I believe this process will take. I once read that every cell in our body changes every seven years. That means we literally become a new person every seven years. Although this process will vary for everyone, I believe that to repent enough and to be humble enough to allow God to change our hearts, that a good length of time to accomplish this significant victory would be seven years. However, the task of becoming perfect even as our beloved Father is perfect will last throughout our lifetime and on into the eternities.

Final Thoughts

It is quite clear to me that for those of us who love God and wish to learn how to live with and love all of God's children, one modification of our behavior may help us to love all of God's children more than anything else we may do. What is this secret of the ages? We are the ones who get to forgive everyone for their trespasses against us and that includes even our enemies and those who persecute us and despitefully use us. It is up to us to make the first move and not the other fella. Because if we wait for the other individual to come to us and apologize to us and beg our forgiveness, we may be waiting many lifetimes!

We are also the ones who get to apologize and ask forgiveness of others for our mistakes and any unkind feelings even disappointment in the behavior of others we may have. And that is even when the other fella is clearly in the wrong and even when we are falsely accused of that which we did not do. Will we ever be able to forgive ourselves? I answer yes. Because of the infinite atonement of Jesus Christ and by the grace of Christ we can absolutely learn how to forgive ourselves of any past mistakes or transgressions with the exception of but one. Jesus said: "All manner of sin and blasphemy shall be forgiven unto men: but the blasphemy against the Holy Ghost (the unpardonable sin) shall not be forgiven unto men" (Matthew 12: 31, emphasis added).

The ultimate objective for all of God's children is for them to be able to say, "Father not my will, but thine, be done," (Luke 22:42). "For thine is the kingdom, and the power, and the glory, forever. Amen" (Matthew 6:13). God has given us our will, but only when we choose to give our will back to him will our Heavenly Father be able to give us both wisdom and understanding. With that wisdom and understanding and by the marvelous enabling power of the atonement of Jesus Christ, we can begin to practice all of the facets of forgiveness discussed in this book.

Our beloved Savior, Jesus Christ is standing at your proverbial front door waiting to change your heart and forgive you of your sins. Will you open the door to your heart and let him in? The best way I know of to do that is to begin forgiving others for their trespasses against you, to begin asking forgiveness of those you have offended and to have the courage to begin forgiving yourself.

The End

About the Author

Ronald H. Bartalini was born and raised in California. He has written two books of poetry, *"I Like You Because You Make Me Happy."* and, "Whispers and Sounds." He is also the author of, *"My Greatest Love, Missionary Stories from My Life," "Living With and Loving All of God's Children-A Primer For Youth-Musings on Manners and More," "Growing Up in America-A Primer for Youth-Musings on Making Your Dreams Come True and More,* and "Hoppity Moose and the Red Caboose" and "The Little Leaf Tree." He currently resides in Utah.

Captain's Log

Captain's Log